PEARLS

— OF —

VEDIC WISDOM
T O   S U C C E E D

Drop the Ego, Be Liberated; Drop I and Mine, Be Free.

Dr. YOGI DEVARAJ

ARUN KUMAR

VENUGOPALA CV

www.SentientLifeEnergy.com

notionpress
.com

INDIA · SINGAPORE · MALAYSIA

Notion Press

Old No. 38, New No. 6
McNichols Road, Chetpet
Chennai - 600 031

First Published by Notion Press 2018
Copyright © Yogi Devaraj, Arun Kumar, Venugopala CV 2018
All Rights Reserved.

ISBN 978-1-64429-066-8

Contents

Foreword

H.H. Pujya Swami Chidanand Saraswatiji
President, Parmarth Niketan

Dear Divine Souls,

I am so glad to know that Shri Yogi Devarajji, Shri Arun Kumarji and Shri Venugopalaji are bringing forth this invaluable book, entitled "Pearls of Vedic Wisdom to Succeed," in which they have made sincere efforts to share ancient, timeless and vital Vedic concepts in a simple and comprehendible manner. Thereby empowering readers with the keys for leading a happy, peaceful and stress-free life.

I strongly feel that the time has come along with surfing web pages we must not forget to read and reflect upon our ancient and timeless Ved pages. India is a country where knowledge from the web must be combined with wisdom from the Ved. This will ensure that our speed and growth has a direction and is truly sustainable. This will also ensure that our development is one that is in harmony with our environment and is inclusive of all humanity regardless of caste, colour, creed, race, religion and region. Most importantly, we must not just read and know the Vedas but if we must truly live the Vedas.

I, once again, commend their efforts to provide our ancient pearls of wisdom in a condensed, concise and relevant manner in order to encourage and inspire the application of this beautiful knowledge and insight ever present in our Vedic philosophy.

With love and blessings always,
In service of God and humanity,

Swami Chidanand Saraswati
Parmarth Niketan (Rishikesh)

Parmarth Niketan Ashram, PO Swargashram, Rishikesh (Himalayas), Uttarakhand 249304, India
Phone: +91-135 2440070 / +91-135 2440055 Fax: +91-135 2440066
@ www.pujyaswamiji.org swamiji@parmarth.com pujyaswamiji
@ www.parmarth.org parmarthniketan

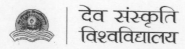

देव संस्कृति
विश्वविद्यालय

विश्वविद्यालय अनुदान आयोग द्वारा मान्यता प्राप्त, राष्ट्रीय मूल्यांकन एवं प्रत्यायन परिषद द्वारा प्रत्यायित एवं आईएसओ 9001:2008 द्वारा प्रमाणित संस्था

मई 16, 2018

आत्मीय बंधु,

आपकी प्रेरक कृति 'Pearls of Vedic Wisdom to Succeed' हमें उपहारस्वरूप मिली। इस स्नेह-सौभाग्य के लिए व्यक्तिगत रूप से स्वयं तथा देव संस्कृति विश्वविद्यालय परिवार आपका हृदय से आभार व्यक्त करता है।

हम अनुभव करते हैं कि जनमानस का भावनात्मक नवनिर्माण करने के लिए जिस विचारक्रान्ति की मशाल इस ज्ञानझरूपी कृति के अन्तर्गत जल रही है उसके प्रकाश में अपने देश, समाज और विश्व का आशाजनक उत्कर्ष सुनिश्चित है।

पूज्य गुरुदेव कहते थे कि नवयुग की चेतना घर-घर पहुँचाने और जन-जन को जागृति का संदेश सुनाने का ठीक यही समय है। इन दिनों हमारी भूमिका युगदूतों जैसी होनी चाहिए। इन दिनों हमारे प्रयास संस्कृति का सेतु बाँधने वाले नल-नील जैसे होने चाहिए। खाई कूदने वाले अंगद की तरह, पर्वत उठाने वाले हनुमान की तरह, यदि पुरुषार्थ न जगे तो भी गिद्ध-गिलहरी की तरह अपने तुच्छ को महान के सम्मुख समर्पित कर सकना तो संभव हो ही सकता है। गोवर्धन उठाते समय यदि हमारी लाठी भी सहयोग के लिए न उठी तो भी स्रष्टा का प्रयोजन पूर्णता तक रुकेगा नहीं, किन्तु पश्चाताप का घाटा हमें ही सहना पड़ेगा।

आज जबकि घायल समाज को राहत देने वाले साहित्य की जरूरत थी, उद्बोधन आवश्यक थे, तब आप द्वारा सृजित पुस्तक भी आशा की किरणें बनकर आई हैं, कारण कि मानव समाज को सदा के लिए दुर्भाग्यग्रस्त नहीं रखा जा सकता। उसे महान आदर्शों के अनुरूप ढलने और बदलने के लिए बलपूर्वक ज्ञानमार्ग से घसीट ले जाना ही होगा। पाप और पतन का युग बदला जाना चाहिए और उसे बदला भी जा सकता है।

चेतना विस्तार की आपकी अग्रणी भूमिका को श्रद्धेय डॉक्टर डॉ० प्रणव पण्ड्या जी एवं श्रद्धेया शैल जीजी ने विश्वमानव के नवनिर्माण में एक क्रान्तिकारी कदम बताया है। उन्होंने आपको अपना विशेष स्नेह एवं आशीर्वाद लिखाया है, कृपया इन्हें ग्रहण करें। परम पूज्य गुरुदेव एवं परम वन्दनीया माताजी का संरक्षण आप तथा परिवारजनों पर सदैव बना रहे ऐसी शुभेच्छाओं के साथ हमारी हार्दिक मंगलकामनाएँ ग्रहण करें।

भवदीय

प्रतिष्ठा में,   ट्रॉमप्र।
श्री योगी देवराज,
श्री अरूण कुमार,   (डॉ० चिन्मय पण्ड्या)
श्री वेणुगोपाल
बेंगलूरू, कर्नाटक।

डॉ. चिन्मय पण्ड्या
प्रति कुलपति (एम.बी.बी.एस, पी.जी.डि, एम.आर.सी. साईक-लंदन)
गायत्रीकुञ्ज-शान्तिकुञ्ज, हरिद्वार-249411. (उत्तराखण्ड)
दूरभाषः 91-1334-261367, 262094 (Extn. 5528) • फैक्सः 91-1334-262095
ई-मेलः provc@dsvv.ac.in • वेबसाइटः www.dsvv.ac.in | www.awgp.org

DEV SANSKRITI
VISHWAVIDYALAYA

Recognized by UGC, Accredited by NAAC and an ISO 9001:2008 Certified Institution

DEAR SOULMATES,   July 19, 2018

We are privileged to receive your inspirational literary work titled "Pearls of Vedic Wisdom to Succeed". For this loveable gesture, I along with the entire community of Dev Sanskriti University take this opportunity to offer our heartfelt gratitude.

We strongly believe that your thought provoking literary work in the form of a torch-bearer of knowledge is guaranteed to illumine and enlighten our society, country and the world and usher in a new golden era of emotional wellbeing and harmonious existence of mankind.

Revered Gurudev had always emphasized that the present time is ripe to carry the message of new-age awakening to every household and to kindle the consciousness of every member of the society. These days we need to assume the roles of goodwill ambassadors building bridges between diverse cultures and uniting the humanity…a task akin to what Nala and Nila carried out (while building the great bridge between Rameswaram and Lanka). Even granting that we mortals may not be able to rise to the exalted levels of industrious Angad (who volunteered to leap over the deep moat surrounding Ravana's palace) or emulating the greatness of Lord Hanuman (who lifted the Sanjeevani Mountain), we should be able to contribute our little might to the greater cause of bridging the humanity almost like the tiny squirrels (unsung little heroes who did their bit in building the bridge to Lanka). There is a saying that our tasks for which our Creator has sent us to this planet would remain unfinished, if we do not lend our support to any good cause.

Nowadays, we need literature to awaken our consciousness and bring succour to our wounded society. It is at these much needed times that your literary work seemingly has brought a ray of hope as if to prove that the humanity cannot be left languishing forever beset with misfortunes. Society has to be lifted and guided towards the path of higher Consciousness. Fallen moral values must be rooted out which is indeed an achievable task.

Revered Dr. Pranav Pandyaji and Revered Shailaji opine that your work is a revolutionary step towards rejuvenating the entire humanity. Kindly accept the love and blessings from them. May the blessings of the Pujya Gurudev, Param Vandaneeya Mathaji be always on you and your families. Kindly accept our good wishes and benedictions.

In praise of:

Yogi Devaraj

Arun Kumar

Venugopala CV

Sincerely

Dr. Chinmay Pandya

Dr. Chinmay Pandya
Pro Vice Chancellor (MBBS, PGDipl, MRCPsych - London)

Gayatrikunj - Shantikunj, Haridwar - 249 411 (Uttarakhand)
Phone: 91-1334-261367, 262094 (Extn. 5528) • **Fax:** 91-1334-262095
Email: provc@dsvv.ac.in • **Website:** www.dsvv.ac.in I www.awgp.org

Foreword by Justice M. N. Venkatachaliah

This book has brought about innovations in the effective treatment of psychological disorders. This is an area of increasing relevance and importance for the alleviations of the personality aberrations of the homo-economicus. Modern man is finding it increasingly difficult to balance his relentless pursuit of worldly goods on the one hand and peace and tranquility of the mind so essential for true happiness on the other. Western science took-up the investigations to understand and de-mystify the function of the human brain. The last decade of the last century (called "the Decade of the Brain") intensified the pursuit of this area.

Wealth, status, authority and power are not evils by themselves. They contribute to the advancement of human welfare and happiness; but they should be regarded only as mere way-side stops in the exciting journey of the exploration of the moral and spiritual dimensions of human personality. "Pearls of Vedic Wisdom to Succeed" is really a tidy Hand Book in helping this process.

– **Padma Vibhushan Sri. M. N. Venkatachaliah**
Retd. Chief Justice of India

Foreword by Scientist Dr. Dillibabu Vijayakumar

The book is packed with useful information to the readers to attain the eternal happiness and to maintain calm and composed mind in all circumstances to lead a stress-free life. Very inspiring, gives good insight on Vedanta. Enlightens us with subtle concepts explained in a most simple way with apt examples. Great attempt in trying to mix the ancient Vedic concepts with the thinking of the modern era making it easy to understand the timeless wisdom. Convincingly explains how to drop the ego and realize the presence of the Sentient Life Energy that is giving us life every moment and also shows us the way to experience this all-important Sentient Life Energy.

Dr. Dillibabu Vijayakumar, Scientist,
Defence Research and Development Organization (DRDO),
Bangalore, India.

Preface

"Pearls of Vedic Wisdom to Succeed" is an honest and sincere attempt to bring out the essential Vedic concepts by explaining them in a simple manner with examples applicable to the present times. This book is not about any faith, belief or religion.

This work is not just for the spiritually oriented. This humble work of ours is also intended for college students, professionals, doctors, engineers, scientists, mathematicians, philosophers and all others who delight in getting their intellect churned.

We believe that the abundant timeless wisdom found in Vedic literature can be used in our day-to-day lives to make our lives peaceful, cheerful and meaningful. The goal of Vedanta is to wipe every sorrowful tear off from every eye and instead make the eyes gleam with love springing from blissful inner peace and abundant joy. The great Vedic masters understood that the very purpose of human life is to live happily, healthily and harmoniously.

Immaculate thinking expounded in Vedic concepts could also be easily applied and adopted in our professions to increase our efficiency, creativity and productivity while making our work more enjoyable and ensuring success in all our endeavors.

This book mainly covers the topics related to *Jnana Yoga* (path of knowledge). That means logic and reason are relied upon to convey the ideas convincingly rather than merely accepting the concepts based on belief and blind faith.

The book intends to cater to three different kinds of readers.

- A curious reader who is interested in getting a comprehensive introduction to the ancient Indian Vedic philosophy and to realize how even in the modern era the time-tested Vedic wisdom could be applied to lead a happy, peaceful and stress-free life. Vedic concepts also help to staunchly face one's challenges and difficulties of life without losing the smile or enthusiasm.

- A sincere seeker who is interested in knowing about the energy that is powering our heart, lungs, eyes, ears, hands, legs, the entire body and is providing us with life every moment. Vedanta calls this energy as 'Chit' meaning Consciousness or Sentience. This book helps one in attaining the ultimate goal of realizing and grasping the life-giving **Sentient Life Energy,** the Self, Awareness, Consciousness or Atman.

- An aspiring and motivated individual with an open mind to explore how Vedic ideas and methods could in fact be used to succeed in attaining the desired goals in any field.

The salient feature of this book is the "Chart of Blissful Life" which is a chart that fits in a single page capturing the quintessence of the vast Vedic philosophy. The chart is unique as it beautifully connects the various important Vedic concepts while being a guide and a ready reckoner for easier understanding.

This is an attempt to cover the Vedic philosophy comprehensively yet crisply and to provide enough information to the readers in a single book. This book tries to elucidate in a lucid manner the pearls contained in the treasure of ancient Vedic literature, some of which are mentioned below.

- Clear clarity, sharp focus, unwavering concentration, channelized energy, relentless effort, deftly overcoming challenges, steadfastly enduring difficulties, burning desire and avid zeal are the essential requirements to succeed in attaining the desired goal in a guaranteed manner.

- Ego is the main culprit responsible for the restlessness of the mind due to endless self-centered thoughts. Ego is the root cause of pain, suffering and worrisome thoughts.

- Ego, the lower self, "i" is the veil over the real and higher Self, Atman, the real "I". Using the sword of Knowledge and Discrimination, the ego should be crucified so that the real Self, Atman could be resurrected.

- Drop the ego to experience Happiness, Peace, Oneness and Unity in Diversity. Vedic philosophy provides the knowledge and the path to emerge successful in dropping the ego.

- Drop the ego to immerse in Blissful Individual Peace thereby gaining the eligibility to contribute towards establishing glorious World Peace

- *Nothing can move or function without the help of energy. Similarly, the heart or lungs or any of the body organs cannot move or function on their own without energy. There is indeed verily a life-giving energy present within every one of us and it is also sentient.*

- *This "Sentient Life Energy" powers all the organs of the body including the subtle organs which are the mind and the intellect.*

- All the energies such as electrical, mechanical, heat, light, etc., are inert, whereas Life Energy is the only sentient energy. The Vedic literature calls it as "Chit" meaning Sentience, Consciousness or Awareness.

- The **Sentient Life Energy** is the Chit Shakti, Chetana, Self, Consciousness, Awareness or Atman.

- Instead of wrongly identifying ourselves with ego, name and form, identifying with the **Sentient Life Energy**, the Self, the Atman and existing as a mass of Consciousness or as a **Silent Awareness** is the Liberation, Freedom and the Ultimate Goal.

The Vedic scholars of ancient times were quite advanced in various fields such as Mathematics, Physics, Chemistry, Astronomy, Grammar, Literature, Architecture, Medicine, etc. However, they were not satisfied with the progress made in the scientific fields alone. They wanted to study, explore and understand the very purpose of human life. They firmly believed that life could not be just a journey from womb to tomb.

Hence, the Vedic scholars embarked on the journey of internal exploration of the human mind in their quest to realize the Truth. Vedic philosophy is not based on a single personality or a single book. Spread across several centuries, various masters have shared their wisdom gained in their enlightened state and contributed to the Vedic literature. The Vedic scholars called it the **"Science of Sciences"**. The knowledge postulated in these works holds true even today and is required more so than ever in this modern era to lead a happy, peaceful and stress-free life.

In this book, we might have used certain words and examples repeatedly to drive home the point. In case if you find the repetition excessive and notice any other flaws we beg your pardon and admit that all those mistakes solely belong to us. If you find anything good, useful and worthy in this book, then the credit wholly belongs to the Vedic literature and the great masters with enlightened minds who relentlessly propounded the Vedic philosophy for the benefit of all of us.

This effort is our humble tribute to the revered masters, great sages, noble souls and enlightened beings, who out of their love and compassion were kind enough to share their vast knowledge and sublime wisdom for the betterment, upliftment and harmonious existence of the entire humanity.

Acknowledgements

With the deepest gratitude, we wish to thank every person who has painstakingly reviewed, encouraged and helped in their capacity to bring out this book successfully.

We would like to wholeheartedly thank a person who did not wish to be mentioned by name but his detailed and thorough reviews of our manuscripts helped immensely.

Our deepest appreciations to Mrs. Pushpa Priyadarshini, her husband Mr. B. Sridhar, Mrs. Shaily Bir and Mr. Kousik Nandy for diligently reviewing many versions and providing valuable comments.

Our sincere appreciations and hearty congratulations to Mehar Simhadri, Technical Lead at Cisco for taking time to review multiple versions and providing valuable comments and in the process having gained the enlightenment. He delightfully acknowledges that reading the book has been a life-changing event. He gleefully says that he can now be in **Silent Awareness** and experience the **Sentient Life Energy** at ease and will.

Our profound gratitude to Mrs. Chandrika Kumar, wife of Arun Kumar and their two sons Ashwin Kumar and Deepak Kumar, Mrs. Anitha, wife of Venugopala, and their two daughters Aishwarya and Mahima for their astounding efforts, meaningful feedback and abundant love and encouragement.

Our heartfelt gratitude to the enlightened, holy and humble man Sri. Parvathappa Guruji for approving our work and showering on us his blessings and well wishes.

Overview of the Blissful Life Chart

"However difficult life may seem, there is always something you can do and succeed at."

– Stephen Hawking

Vedic literature helps a sincere seeker to attain the goal in the spiritual path. The same Vedic concepts are very well applicable to attain the goal in any field or profession or just to lead a happy and peaceful life.

Vedas are a large body of ancient texts that are the origin of Vedic philosophy. There are four Vedas, Rig Veda, Yajur Veda, Sama Veda and Atharva Veda. Each Veda has been further classified into four text types – the Samhitas (mantras), the Aranyakas (rituals and ceremonies), the Brahmanas (commentaries on rituals and ceremonies) and the Upanishads (texts discussing meditation, philosophy and knowledge).

There are around 108 Upanishads out of which 10 are considered to be the principal Upanishads.

Vedic philosophy comprises of Vedas, Upanishads, Brahma Sutras, Bhagavad-Gita, Bhagavatha, Yoga Vasishta, Patanjali Yoga Sutras, several monumental works done by great scholars like Shankaracharya, Sureshvaracharya, Vidyaranya, Alwars (12 enlightened saints devoted to Lord Vishnu), Shaiva Nayanars (63 enlightened saints devoted to Lord Shiva), Ramanuja, Madhvacharya, etc.

"Chart of Blissful Life" is the unique highlight of this book as the single chart in a single page captures the essence of Vedanta and brings forth the pearls of wisdom advocated by Vedas, Upanishads, ancient Indian texts, great Saints and the wise Acharyas (Teachers).

Let us examine the chart in brief to get a bird's eye view. At first glance, the chart may be overwhelming. We request the readers to take it easy, be patient and do not try to understand it right away. Later in the book, we shall delve deep into the components contained in the chart, analyze and understand each one of them in detail. While explaining each individual component, that portion of the chart containing the component is provided at the beginning of each explanation.

By the time the book is completely read the explanations help one to understand the chart in its entirety. As the clarity of the Vedic knowledge is gained, one would become equipped to do **Svadhyaya** (self-study and introspection) and **Svanubhava** (self-experience and understanding). The Vedic concepts guide and help us to find the solutions and make the required changes in life to lead a meaningful, successful, pleasant and blissful life.

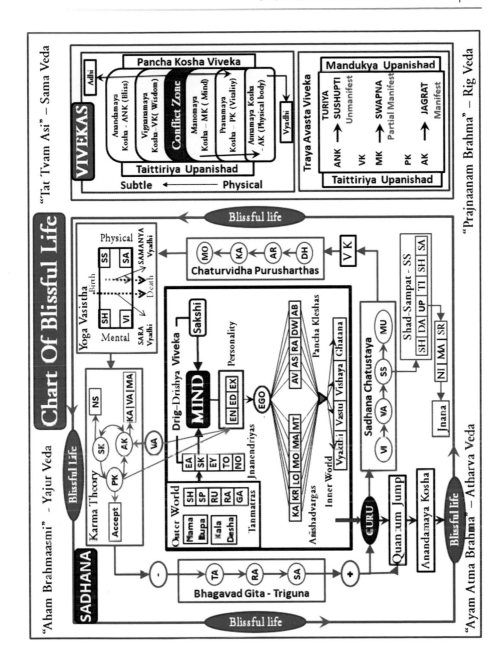

The chart essentially is made up of three parts, "**The Mind**", "**Vivekas**" (Reasoning) and "**Sadhana**" (Effort).

The Mind

The first part of the chart is the box at the center of the chart titled "Mind", explains the composition of the mind, the nature of the mind and the factors that influence the working of the mind.

The Zen philosophy says that *"Mind is nothing but a mischief"*. One of the great sages of the twentieth century who lived in the South Indian State, Tamil Nadu, Sri Ramana Maharshi, says, *"Mind is nothing but the thought"*.

The stimuli and inputs are provided by the "Outer World" to the mind. The analysis and interpretations of the thinking mind contribute to the modifications of the "Inner World". The thinking of the mind is influenced by one's personality, ego, feelings, emotions, biases, afflictions, beliefs, predispositions, etc. Understanding the working of the mind in detail helps us to reduce unnecessary thoughts, lessen the intensity of our worries, calm our mind and live the life cheerfully.

Vivekas – Reasoning

The second part is the box in the extreme right, titled "Vivekas", help us with the reasonings required to understand how the human body, mind and intellect are integrated, the nature of human existence and the factors affecting the human behaviors.

Viveka means reasoning. The Vedic masters provide many different reasonings to comprehend and strive to reach the ultimate goal which is realizing the **Sentient Life Energy**, Self, Consciousness, or to simply "Know Thyself".

Vivekas throw light on the nature of the ego and how it affects the human behavior. The three states of human existence are explored, which are waking, dream and deep sleep states. The study is made to understand the true nature of the human being at the core. We all know that nothing in this world can move without the help of energy. Our heart beats, lungs expand and contract and all other body organs function. Vivekas question whether "can these organs function on their own?" thereby helping us realize the presence of the **Sentient Life Energy** that is powering and operating the body, the mind and the intellect.

Sadhana – Effort

"Sadhana" means effort, which is putting all the learnings into action to achieve the desired goal.

The third part of the chart is the bigger and outer rectangle in the center of the chart. It has Guru as the locus, should be traversed counter-clockwise and contains components illustrating various Vedic concepts that need to be imbibed and implemented for successfully leading a blissful and stress-free life. One would have to do the traversal many times, each time with more improved comprehension, better understanding and more intense practicing of the ideals and concepts taught by the Guru.

With the help of the grace within oneself, one comes in contact with a Guru who shows the ways and the means to accomplish our goal. Guru could be a person, books, discourses, videos, etc. But remember, Guru can only talk the talk, and it is we who have to walk the walk.

After several traversals in the path shown by the Guru, each time intensifying and perfecting the Sadhana, we get the eligibility to make a Quantum Jump to achieve the ultimate goal and succeed in abiding in a continuous blissful state.

Chapter 1
The Mind

"The mind is like an iceberg; it floats with only a small portion being visible above the water and the rest is hidden beneath."

— Sigmund Freud

ॐ ॐ ॐ

Om Sahanaa Vavatu
Sahanau Bhunaktu
Saha Veeryam Karavaa Vahai
Tejasvi Nau Vadhee Tamastu Maa Vidvishaa Vahai
Om Shaanti Shaanti Shaantihi

Om, May we all be protected.
May we all be nourished (with knowledge).
May we work together with energy and vigor.
May our study be enlightening and let there be no poison of hatred
or animosity amongst us.
Om, Peace (in me), Peace (in world), Peace (in all forces that act
upon us)

ॐ ॐ ॐ

About the Mind

"The mind…can make a heaven of hell, a hell of heaven."

– John Milton

The Mind is the seat for the world of thoughts, feelings, attitudes, beliefs, and imaginations. Mind matters most as it is the most important instrument that is responsible for learning, creativity, innovation and for that matter everything we achieve in this world.

According to the Vedic literature, the thinking instrument (Antahkarana) consists of Manas (Mind), Buddhi (Intellect), Chitta (Memory) and Ahamkara (Ego). Manas, the mind processes the input from the sensory organs and is also responsible for desires and thoughts. Buddhi, the intellect knows, decides, judges and discriminates. Chitta, the memory is the storehouse of the impressions. Ahamkara, the ego provides the identity through which the individuality emerges as "I", which further gives rise to the feelings of me and mine.

There are several components that affect and influence the Mind and each one of them is explained in detail in the subsequent sections.

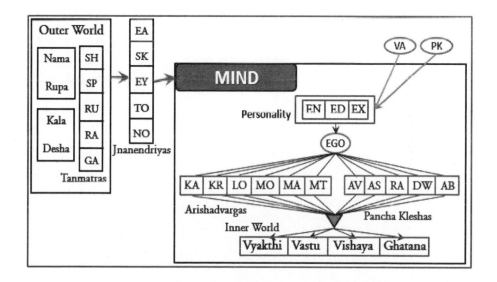

Outer World comprises of the physical world we live in and interact with. The inputs from the Outer World are received by the mind through the five sense organs (Jnanendriyas).

The mind of each individual interprets the inputs differently because each one has a unique Personality, Ego, Arishadvargas (emotions and passions) and Pancha Kleshas (five afflictions of the mind). The assimilations and interpretations of the mind affect our Inner World which influences our thoughts.

Mind's nature is to generate various kinds of thoughts. The Internet search reveals that each day an average person has thousands of thoughts, most of which are repetitions. Psychologists observe that more than 70% of our thoughts are negative and redundant. Too many negative thoughts adversely affect the inner world causing fear, anxiety and stress. That's why it is essential to have a positive attitude, nourish and cherish positive thoughts for mental peace, cheerfulness and positive results. There is a Sanskrit proverb, *"Yad bhavam, tad bhavati"*, which means "We become what we think".

Understanding the functioning of the mind intricately and gaining the ability to dispassionately analyze the thoughts can help one make great strides towards happy and stress-free living.

Should we conclude that the mind is really the most important thing for a human being? Or is it not so? Does a thing called mind really exist? We shall try to find answers to these interesting and contradictory questions as we embark upon this journey.

Inner World

"It is still breathtaking to me to watch people bring love, preciousness and kindness to their inner world, allowing the light of God to shine through their eyes so that the beauty of their soul can come forth."

– Debbie Ford

The inner world of the mind is formed by processing the input received from the outer world. Our feelings, emotions, beliefs and pre-dispositions contribute towards the mind's interpretation of the inputs. This inner world influences the innumerous thoughts that are generated unceasingly in the mind. According to Sigmund Freud, the inner world comprises of Conscious Mind, Preconscious Mind and Unconscious Mind.

Though the thoughts are innumerous, interestingly every single thought always revolves around **Vyakti** (Person), **Vastu** (Object), **Vishaya** (Subject) and **Ghatana** (Incident). Though these are clearly the objects of the Outer World, they are the subjects of our thoughts which constitute our Inner World. Generally, thoughts about the Vyakti (person) and Vastu (object) are more dominant and frequent as invariably they are the subjects of the most number of conversations.

Inner World			
Vyakthi	Vastu	Vishaya	Ghatana

Swami Chinmayananda says that thought has to have an object. Without an object, there is no thought. Just read the following words. Mahatma Gandhi, Eiffel Tower, Electricity, Attack on World Trade Center. Reading those words might have generated some thoughts about them, but before reading those words, you were definitely not thinking about them. That means, not all the objects of the world constitute our thoughts. Only those objects that we become conscious of, become our thoughts. By making you deliberately read those words, they were brought into your Consciousness and hence thoughts occurred about those objects. Thus, Consciousness coupled with an object becomes a thought.

$$Consciousness + Object = Thought$$

Using simple arithmetic, the above equation can be rewritten as
$$Consciousness = Thought - Object$$

From the above equation, we see that to experience only the Consciousness, we need to have a thought without any object. Can we have a thought without an object? Let us try to find the answer to this intriguing question as we go further.

Vyakti – Person

Vyakti (Person) means all the individuals whom we communicate and interact with. It is common to have positive or negative thoughts while thinking about a person.

At times, we are plagued with negative thoughts while thinking about a **Vyakti** (person) because the person might have insulted us or offended us or hurt us or we might have developed too much hatred about that person. In such situations, we just need to remember that a few years back we might have felt just as strongly about some other person which are no longer bothering us now. Similarly, the present negative thoughts which are causing us agony are also impermanent, will definitely pass and would even might look silly if we happen to ponder about them in the future, say a few years from now. It is agreed that it is easier said than done to get away from the worrying thoughts immediately. But knowing the fact that the present worry too is temporary just like the several worries we might have had in the past helps to reduce the intensity of the current worries and eventually become free and relieved.

Basically, instead of thinking and worrying, it calls for calm and clear analysis. For example, if our boss is being unreasonable and hurting us, we need to sit down and explore all the options available to us. If he is genuine, then we need to correct ourselves and try to improve our capability and efficiency. If the boss's objections are not valid, there is always an option of switching to a new department or a new job in another organization. If the boss is a habitual whiner, try ignoring without taking it too personally or explore the option of approaching the higher-ups to bring about a change which may be agreeing on better ways of working and improving the environment.

The critical thing to be remembered is that we cannot change others, but we can definitely change ourselves and our way of thinking. If we cannot get away from a person, then talking openly about the issues and coming to an agreement after considering each other's point of view should be attempted. If that does not work, according to Swami Anubhavananda, accepting the person as is for who they are and moving on is the only way for stress-free and peaceful living. Scott Adams, creator of Dilbert Comic Strip, in his book "God's Debris" says, *"It is futile to look for someone who has no flaws, or someone who is capable of significant change; that sort of person exists only in our imaginations"*.

As we experience thoughts about a **Vyakti** (person), in the same way, we also could be the subject of thought of somebody else and could be influencing them either positively or negatively. In the essay "On Saying Please", A.G. Gardiner, emphasizes the importance of good manners, politeness, social concerns, etc. and illustrates how a discourteous, uncivil, boorish and rude behavior sets off negative chain reactions affecting people around us. We have a responsibility towards our environment and ensure that as a **Vyakti** (person) we radiate happiness all around rather than causing hate and distress.

It would be appropriate here to recollect a narration by Dale Carnegie in one of his books. You go to a church to attend a funeral. People have formed a line to approach the coffin and pay their last respects. On the stage, three people are getting ready to speak a few words about the departed soul. One is the son of the dead person, another is a close friend and the third is the Father of the church. As your turn arrives to pay your last respects, you place the wreath and peep into the coffin to have a last look. To your shock and horror, you find that the dead person is none other than you. Now you decide what those three people on the stage should be talking about the deceased which is you. Keeping in mind whatever we want those people on the stage to be talking, we can start living as that kind of successful **Vyakti** (person) from now on.

We have positive thoughts when we think of a national hero, famous statesman, gifted sportsman, favorite actor, etc. We feel much more positivity when the nice thoughts are about a friend, relative, child or spouse, as the person happens to be close to us and emotionally connected. The highest state of positive thoughts is experienced along with pleasant feelings when we think about a **Vyakti** (person) whom we deeply love. For example, when a person deep in romance is thinking about the partner, a great state of mind accompanied with euphoric feelings are experienced. One wants to be in that state endlessly, thinking about the lover and forgetting the external world completely. Hunger is not felt, time loses relevance, irrespective of the location or place the passionate feelings persist and any other thing that disturbs this pleasant state is found to be irritating.

Regarding love, the British philosopher Bertrand Russell opines, *"Those who have never known the deep intimacy and the intense companionship of mutual love have missed the best thing that life has to give"*.

As human beings are social animals, love comes naturally and is expressed in many ways as motherly love, fatherly love, love between siblings, love in friendship, love in companionship, etc. This phenomenon of experiencing a highly pleasant state while thinking about a person who is immensely loved is also seen in the Bhaktas (devotees) immersed in Bhakti (devotion). The Bhaktas personify their God in human form as a **Vyakti** (person) and try to continuously remain in the loving thought of that God in the human form. This is called Bhakti Yoga (Path of Devotion) and it does not require too much logic. Instead, it requires steadfast faith, unflinching belief and unconditional love towards God. Bhakti Rasa (taste of devotion) is expressed and experienced using five Bhavas (Feelings or Emotions or Attitudes). Bhaktas are free to choose whichever bhava or multiple bhavas they like for expressing their devotion.

- In **Shanta Bhava** (Calmness), the devotee is in a calm and blissful state, loving and thinking about God. Generally, saints are in this state.

- In **Dasya Bhava** (Servitude), the devotee assumes to be a very obedient and blessed servant and considers God as the master. Sri Hanuman used this bhava to worship his Lord Sri Rama.

- In **Sakhya Bhava** (Friendship), God is treated as a very close friend. Cowherds in Brindavan and the great archer Arjuna had this bhava towards Lord Krishna.

- In **Vatsalya Bhava** (Parental Love), God is considered as a child and loved. Devaki and Yashoda loved Lord Krishna as their child.

- In **Madhurya Bhava** (Romance), God is considered as a partner and the devotee indulges in an intense romance with God. Radha and Aandal considered Lord Krishna and Lord Ranga respectively as their romantic partners and liked to be continuously in the loving thought of their Lord.

These are the normal bhavas (feelings) we experience in our everyday lives while interacting with our parents, children, spouse, friends, boss, etc. and the Bhaktas use the same natural feelings to express their devotion to their beloved Lord.

Vastu - Object

Vastu (Object) is a thing which may be present in the physical world, materialistic world or mental world. The gross objects like mountains, rivers, trees, city, place, etc., are the objects belonging to the physical world. Wealth, property, phone, car, resort, restaurant, etc., are part of the materialistic world. Mind, intellect, memory, ego are the subtle objects belonging to the mental world.

We seek repeated enjoyment from the materialistic things and assign a status to the materialistic possessions like wealth, property, car, house, etc. The desire to want and accumulate more possessions forms the greed. If a thing cannot be attained, it becomes a source of worry. Satisfaction and contentment with the existing possessions lead to positive thoughts and happiness. The Greek philosopher Plato also concurs by saying, *"The greatest wealth is to live contented with little"*.

We discussed how the tendency of the mind to think about a Vyakti (person) is used in Bhakti Yoga. In Jnana Yoga (Path of Knowledge), the Sentient Life Energy or the Awareness or the Consciousness which is the ultimate goal is conceived or cognized as a Vastu (a thing or an object) and the seeker practices to remain thinking and contemplating on it continuously. In Tamil language, it is called "Param Porul" meaning "Ultimate Vastu" or "Ultimate Thing".

Though the word "Vastu" or "thing" is used here for Consciousness, Upanishads call it ineffable, indescribable, a thing that cannot be explained in words, but should be contemplated upon and then experienced. Unlike Bhakti Yoga, Jnana Yoga employs logic and requires sharp intellect to understand it. First, one should learn by reading or hearing about the Jnana Yoga, then question, contemplate, understand clearly without any doubt and finally after getting completely convinced, pursue and practice it with conviction. Let's examine how the realization of Self or Consciousness is attempted in Jnana Yoga.

When we use the language like 'my car', 'my phone', 'my pen', etc., it means I am the owner. When the word 'My' is used it means I am the owner of an object and the object is the owned. In other words, the owner and the owned are clearly distinct and cannot be the same.

My smartphone is an object owned by me and I am its owner. But I am not the phone itself. My house is owned by me and I am its owner.

I am not the house itself. My little finger on my right hand is mine and I am its owner. I am not the little finger itself. The same logic can be applied to the right hand, both the hands, both the legs and for that matter the entire body along with its internal and external organs which we refer to as "My Body". Hence the body is owned by me and I am the owner. I cannot be the body itself. What about our name? The name also we refer to it as "My Name" which is just a label given to the body for identification and transaction. When the body itself is discarded as "Not I" then the name loses its relevance. All the internal elements such as mind, intellect, etc., we call it "My Mind", "My Intellect". By the same logic, I am the owner of the mind and not the mind itself.

I am not my body. I am not my mind. I am not my intellect. Then who am I? Let us find out. Our heart beats, lungs expand and contract and all other organs function. It is an insult to common sense to think that these functions are happening on their own. Can anything in this world move or function on its own? No, it requires the help of some energy for anything to move or function. All of us do possess such an energy which powers all the body organs, the mind and the intellect. The Vedas say that unlike other energies which are *"inert"* this life energy is *"sentient"* which means it has Consciousness or rather it is Consciousness itself.

According to the Vedas, the real "I", the owner of the body, mind and intellect is the Sentient Life Energy which is the Consciousness. Consciousness is also known by several other names such as Chetana (Energy), Chit Shakti (Sentient Energy), Prajna (Consciousness, Awareness), Life Force or Life Energy or Life Principle (without which the body dies and starts rotting), Indweller (dweller within the body), Knower, Perceiver, Thinker, Seer, Experiencer, Sakshi (Witness), Self, Atman (Soul), Brahman (Almighty Energy), Kutastha (Unchanging), etc. Meditation is practiced to realize this Consciousness.

Meditation is nothing but single-pointed concentration. Sadhu Om, a disciple of Sri Ramana Maharshi, in his book "The Path of Sri Ramana", says that the way a meditation should be done is by "paying attention" to the Consciousness and not "thinking" about the Consciousness. Paying attention means just a simple observation or being in awareness without doing any mentation or thinking. It is important to understand clearly the difference between observation and thinking.

For example, when we look at a flower, we just look at it. There is nothing to think. Only if we compare it with some other flower, want to know how and where it is grown or do any such things other than merely looking at it, then the thinking happens. While just looking at it in the initial few seconds when there are "no thoughts" we are just paying attention without doing any thinking.

In the same way, for a few seconds, if we watch the swinging pendulum of a clock, there is nothing to think and we are just paying attention or in observation. The important thing to note here is that while paying attention or doing observation, the mind does not have to think. Only if we get interested in different thoughts such as whose clock it is, how old it is, how is the pendulum swinging, what is its length, etc., it is then the thinking starts happening. For just observation, no thinking is required, no mentation is necessary.

Equipped with the clear understanding of the meaning of observation, let us try to make the direct enquiry of Self through meditation as prescribed by Sri Ramana Maharshi. The meditation is done by sitting in a comfortable posture in a calm place, closing the eyes and with single-pointed concentration, one should try to observe (pay attention to) the breath. No controlling or holding of breath, it is just a simple observation of the breath. Meditation is said to be done correctly if two things are observed or experienced. One is the observation of inhalation and exhalation of breath and the second one is the experience of the enormous silence. At this juncture, please take a pause, re-read this paragraph, understand it clearly, try to do the suggested meditation for a few minutes, observe the breath with full concentration and experience the silence.

Continue the same meditation, this time concentrating only on the silence and be casual about the breath. As it is "My Breath", the breath cannot be I. Just allow the breathing to happen automatically on its own accord and try to experience the silence fully. At this stage, a very simple, yet a key realization has to happen. Instead of saying "I am experiencing the silence", it can be said that "I have become aware of the silence" or "I am in awareness of the silence". That's it. I am just aware of the silence in that meditative state. That awareness is very much the Consciousness, I or the Self. All we need to do is do nothing and "just be" in the silence or "just exist" in the silence or be in **Silent Awareness.**

Experiencing the silent beatitude is the key. The silence is nothing but the nature of Awareness as Awareness does not make any noise. If we take any energy, say magnetic energy or gravitational energy, its nature is silence. In the same way, the nature of Awareness, the Life Energy is also silence. The nature of fire is heat. But heat is not fire. In the same way, the nature of Awareness is silence. But silence is not Awareness. Hence, the silence also can be ignored and continuing just being in the state of resplendent Awareness and experiencing its bliss is the goal. This being in Silent Awareness is said to be the real human nature which is marked by silence and purity and is considered to be the pristine form of human existence.

When being in the state of Awareness or Consciousness, the mind is quiet and allows the Awareness to shine through. After constant practice, the mind gets habituated to pay attention to this ethereal Awareness. The mind is allowing Awareness to be aware of itself without thinking about any other Vastu or object. This being in Silent Awareness is what can be called as thought without an object. So, for the question can we have a thought without an object, a Jnana Yogi emphatically proclaims "Yes! We Can!!".

Vishaya - Topic

Vishaya (Subject) is a topic, idea, theme, subject or a concept. **Vishaya** is a computer programmer thinking about an algorithm, a scientist thinking hard to frame a hypothesis, a mathematician analyzing or deducing a theorem, an engineer thinking about the tasks that have to be performed, an army general brainstorming on how to fight the battle, a doctor contemplating on the symptoms exhibited by the patient and trying to decide on the treatment needed, an employee deliberating on various points that could be used for the upcoming presentation, etc.

To think deeply on a **Vishaya** (subject), the intellect is relied upon and made more use of. As Swami Chinmayananda says, animals have fully developed body and mind, but no intellect. Hence animals live with their four basic instincts: eating, sleeping, fear (helps in fight or flight) and procreation. Human beings are not satisfied to live with just the animal instincts because along with the body and the mind, human beings are endowed with a fully developed intellect. Humans like to be sapient, sagacious, rationalize, theorize, judge and discern the good from the bad, right from the wrong, all because of the intellect.

Thinking about simple things like the next day at work, what tasks need to be attended to and in what order, constitute **Vishaya** (topic) and these thoughts are clearly not about Vyakti (person) or Vastu (object). Everyone has thoughts about Vishaya (topic) on a daily basis. If these thoughts are a little out of the ordinary, then they get termed as ideas or strategies or concepts. Endeavour to come up with brilliant ideas, tactful strategies, extraordinary concepts, etc., leads to creativity. There is a saying, *"Good thoughts precede great deeds. Great deeds precede success"*.

When a good idea works and also gets appreciated, one gets a sense of accomplishment which is extremely satisfying. In the corporate world, a leader is considered good if one can ensure an overall sense of accomplishment in the entire team by assigning the right kind of tasks to each of the team members. Assigning not so challenging tasks to the highly skilled people results in wastage of time and resources with very little job satisfaction. Assigning non-trivial tasks to somebody whose skill level is not adequate, results in poor quality, slipped deadlines and diminishes the confidence and morale of the whole team. That's why assigning the right kind of tasks to right kind of people irrespective of their title or position or experience but purely based on their knowledge and skill level, allows everybody to succeed and experience the satisfaction that comes from the sense of accomplishment.

This sense of accomplishment feeling is tapped into by the successful social media applications such as Facebook, Twitter, WhatsApp, etc. For example, if one finds a nice quotation, posts the same on Facebook and if the person gets a large number of "likes" then there is a sense of achievement. It does not matter that the quotation is not an original creation and belongs to somebody else.

When our thought on a Vishaya (topic) is great and innovative, we feel good and when several people appreciate it, we feel elated as our pride is flattered due to the recognition and appreciation. Since time immemorial, mankind has been engaged in creativity, invention and discovery which makes us ponder that there has to be a much more profound reason than the mere presence of the sense of achievement and appreciation. When the Vishaya (topic) thought is much more profound and intense to unearth or prove a path-breaking concept, then the joy is not obtained from "I did it" feeling or from others' appreciation. If the concept is complicated enough, then others may not be even able to understand to appreciate and any appreciation without understanding the idea entirely is hollow and does not provide joy.

Then where is the real joy derived from when a new concept is proven to work? From the concept itself. Just finally seeing the concept work, gives sheer delight to the inventor after toiling tirelessly for years, enduring multiple failures and challenges. The sense of doership (I did it) is not present. Creative and innovative concepts are selfless and non-materialistic. Hence conceiving great ideas and successfully implementing them gives unadulterated bliss for people like Marconi, Thomas Edison, Graham Bell, James Watt, Wright Brothers, Alfred Nobel, etc. The point gets well illustrated when we study the story of Archimedes where once he discovered and understood the Buoyancy

Principle while in the bathtub, he was so thrilled that he got up and started running around naked, shouting "Eureka" without paying attention to his body or his clothes.

Creative work is not just a source of joy but is an ocean of bliss and this is the basis of Karma Yoga. Swami Vivekananda talking about the Karma Yoga says, *"Take up one idea. Make that one idea your life; dream of it; think of it; live on that idea. Let the brain, the body, muscles, nerves, every part of your body be full of that idea, and just leave every other idea alone. This is the way to success"*.

When the mind is relentlessly engaged in conceiving a non-trivial concept and is proved by following it up with a successful execution, the joy derived is unmatched and provides us a long-lasting satisfaction. This is another reason why the care should be taken to distribute tasks according to one's skill level, capacity and capability, so that all are able to complete their tasks and everyone is enabled to taste the joy of success. Franklin D. Roosevelt says, *"Happiness lies in the joy of achievement and the thrill of creative effort"*.

Leaders implementing this secret would ensure that their team members are eager to jump out of bed every day to show up at work and get jubilantly immersed in solving the challenges. A great leader not only enjoys the work leading by example, but also inspires others to become self-motivated and enjoy their work, makes the spirit *"Work is Worship"* spring to life and the work becomes play.

Ghatana - Incident

Ghatana means Event or Incident. Just like other objects of thought, **Ghatana** (event) also can contribute to positive or negative thoughts, feelings and emotions.

We are anguished when we think about events like Attack on World Trade Center, World Wars, Jallianwala Bagh Massacre, Bombing of Hiroshima and Nagasaki, etc., which have brought an avalanche of untold miseries upon humanity. We are delighted when we think about events like the tearing down of the Berlin Wall, nations gaining independence from colonial rule, ending of apartheid in South Africa, etc. The historic event of Neil Armstrong stepping on the moon got immortalized when he said to the then President John Kennedy, *"That's one small step for man, one giant leap for mankind"*.

In our personal lives too, events happen that can leave a lasting imprint. The day of our graduation, our first date, the day when our first baby was born, etc., leave positive and pleasant memories in us. An embarrassing situation, the moment where we happened to become the butt of a joke, death of a loved one, etc., are some events that cause negative and disturbing thoughts.

For some people, some events could turn out to be life-changing. It is said that the tennis great Roger Federer was devastated by the sudden death of his Aussie tennis coach Peter Carter in a car accident. Peter coached Federer from the age of 9 to 18. Federer loved his coach so much that the tragic event had a forceful impact on him, made him strengthen his resolve, badly wanted to win his first grand slam to dedicate to his departed coach, upped his game and the rest, as they say, is history. He is now the winner of 20 grand slams and still going strong.

In the case of Thomas Alva Edison, being a hyperactive child and prone to distraction was considered as a nuisance by his teachers. They conveyed their opinions to his mother Nancy, who did not take this event lightly. She inherently knew the genius hidden in her child and took him out of school to provide education at home. The result, the world got blessed with one of the greatest prolific inventors who received over two thousand patents worldwide for his inventions.

There are several such Ghatana or incidents which have catapulted ordinary beings into great masters.

Prince Siddhartha went on to become the great Gautama Buddha after seeing the four sights, an old man, a sick man suffering from disease, a dead body and a mendicant monk.

Ashoka, the Mauryan Emperor, in the aftermath of the dreadful war of Kalinga won by him in 262 BCE, on witnessing the ghastly bloodbath, gruesome carnage, immense pain and agony, had a change of heart and fully embraced Buddhism. Ramesh Mohapatra, in his "Military History of Orissa", captures this incident as, *"No wars in the annals of history has changed the heart of the victor from one of wanton cruelty to that of exemplary piety as this one".*

Ramana Maharshi (1879–1950), one of the greatest sages of our modern era, one day at the age of 16, due to the death of a relative was stricken by the fear of his own death. This event compelled him to conduct an in-depth enquiry in absolute loneliness. He emerged triumphant in his self-enquiry, attained self-realization and renounced the world. He became a great saint attracting a large number of devotees every day by showering his love and wisdom.

In all the above instances we see that even challenging, trying, distressing events, with the help of a positive outlook, got converted into life-changing, serendipitous events.

The war of Kalinga changed the heart of the emperor Ashoka. The British philosopher Paul Brunton in his book "The Spiritual Crisis of Man" laments that the two world wars did not bring about the much-required change in the hearts and minds of the modern generation.

Inner World Summary

In our Inner World, we always harbor positive or negative thoughts about Vyakti (person), Vastu (object), Vishaya (topic) and Ghatana (incident). Of all, the thoughts about Vyakti are the most. Even when we think about the other three, quite often they may be associated with a Vyakti. Similarly, there may be an interconnection with other thoughts also, say when we think about Vishaya or Ghatana it may be linked to a Vastu and vice versa.

We are supposed to "love" all Vyakti (person), but quite often we tend to "make use" of them. Ironically when we are only supposed to "make use" of all Vastu (object), we fall in "love" with them.

Due to the mental makeup shaped by the Inner World for a given circumstance, the responses of different people would not be the same. Let us consider some examples.

We sometimes find a particular Vyakti (person) very difficult to work with, but some others might admire the same person and love working with that person.

Some people might crave to possess a Vastu (object) say a particular necklace, but some others might be utterly disinterested in it.

Some may easily grasp a particular Vishaya (topic), yet some others may find it difficult and not be able to understand it even after repeated attempts.

If somebody climbing up to a podium to give a presentation happens to trip and fall, might feel so embarrassed, start sweating profusely and could find it difficult to remember the points and struggle to make a decent presentation. Somebody else in the same situation might get up, dust off the clothes, go ahead and make a spellbound presentation and might in fact even mention about the fall during the speech and laugh it off.

In all the above instances we see that for a given circumstance different people react differently. So, there is no problem with the outer world. The problem lies in the way we perceive, interpret, react and respond.

Most of the time, sitting calmly, watching our own worrying thoughts and carefully analyzing them can help us get over them and move on with the life wearing a smile. *"We don't see things as they are, rather we see them as we are"*. In the play Hamlet, Shakespeare says, *"There is nothing either good or bad but thinking makes it so"*.

Personality

"We are all born with a unique genetic blueprint, which lays out the basic characteristics of our personality as well as our physical health and appearance… And yet, we all know that life experiences do change us."

– Joan D. Vinge

We all are born with certain inherent characteristics, qualities, capabilities, traits and tendencies. As we grow up, the inputs we receive contribute to molding our personality.

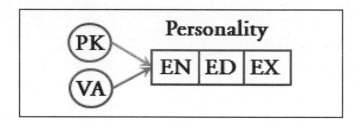

The factors that shape our personality are **Prarabdha Karma** (PK), **Vasanas** (VA), **Environment** (EN), **Education** (ED), and **Experience** (EX). Each component of personality is unique for every individual and their combination again makes it unique. Hence each person's personality is unique. All the elements mentioned combine to shape one's views, opinions, beliefs, predispositions, etc. Personality is an "angle" from which a person views and hence the same thing is viewed, perceived and comprehended by the mind differently for each individual.

Prarabdha Karma (PK)

Vedic philosophy says that everybody is born with **Prarabdha Karma** (PK) which determines all kinds of physical attributes such as the color of the skin, the physique with which the baby is born with and is likely to acquire as it grows. PK is the reason for perfection or defect in the physical faculties such as vision, auditory functions, etc., qualities, capabilities, tendencies, likes and dislikes the child is going to exhibit as it grows up. PK is also responsible for the place and the parents to whom the child is born, the cultural and educational background of the family, the environment in which the child grows up, the kind of teachers, relatives, friends and people the child is likely to attract and interact with and the varied experiences, both good and bad the child is destined to undergo. In short, **Prarabdha Karma** (PK) according to Vedic philosophy, is the effect, fruit or result of the past deeds or actions of the previous births, which are ready to be experienced in the present birth.

Naturally, the question arises, what is the proof that there were previous births before the current birth? To answer this, Sri Chandrasekharendra Saraswati Swamiji (1894–1994), the Sage of Kanchi asks us to just pay a visit to the maternity ward of a hospital and take a look at all the babies born within that week. One would quickly observe that not all the babies are born alike. One is hale and healthy and another is born with a deformity; one born to wealthy parents and another born to parents in utter poverty; one very beautiful and another with some disability; etc. For that matter even, twins may look alike but would differ in their physical and mental capabilities.

Why this difference among the innocent babies born almost around the same time? Let us assume that there were no previous births and this is the only birth. If one believes in God, then God cannot be so partial and unfair to the children who have committed no sin and are taking birth for the very first time. God is supposed to be the epitome of mercy, an apostle of justice and should be showering love equally on all the children. But when we see such a blatantly harsh differentiation made right at the birth on hapless innocent children, then such an unfair God cannot be God at all as it completely violates the definition of a God who is supposed to be impartial, caring, loving and merciful.

If a person is an atheist and also does not believe in previous births then instead of God, Nature has to take the blame for this cruel fate dished out at the birth itself. Yet we know from our experience that Nature does not differentiate and treats everybody the same. Sun shines the same for everybody, air does not provide more oxygen for some and deny it for others, fire does not burn only a few and be cool to others, and water quenches the thirst without any disparity. Nature is the same for everybody and without any discrimination always upholds the law *"As you sow, so you reap"*.

Thus, if we assume that this is the only birth, it fails to provide adequate and convincing logical explanation for so much difference meted out at the time of birth itself. The only reasonable explanation that seems to perfectly fit for this drama unfolding right from the time of birth is the Prarabdha Karma (PK) which is nothing but the result of some of the past deeds that are ready to be experienced in the current birth. Later in the book, there is a separate section on Karma Theory where we shall explore the nature of karmas in more detail.

Vedic philosophy never forces anybody to take any explanation as a matter of faith; instead, it insists and encourages to question every explanation, decipher, analyze, contemplate and understand. Vedas never give any reasoning out of the blue, in fact, they are completely based on the prevailing laws of Nature and the inferences derived out of them. It is crucial to register this particular point which is that the Vedic conclusions are based very much on the laws of Nature which we experience in our day-to-day lives.

Nobody can deny that what we are today is because of the deeds we have committed in the past. For example, if I graduated today, it automatically implies that I have undergone the degree course for the prescribed 3–4 years preceded by 12 years at school starting from the primary. If I have completed building a house, it means that for the past several months I have been busy with the tasks needed to build the house. If there is a profit or loss in the stocks now, it is because of the investments made in the past. It should be clear from the above examples that what we are today is because of our own past deeds and what we want to be in the future gets determined by the thoughts and actions we are going to undertake in the present. Prarabdha Karma (PK) is derived from the same logic and states that what we are now, including from the time of our birth, is because of the deeds we have done in the past.

Now let us consider some extraordinary capabilities displayed by some at very tender age. Mozart was able to compose divine music when he was just 4 years. Mandolin Srinivas showed his expertise with the mandolin at the age of 6. Veena Gayathri gave a masterful public performance at the age of 9. Carl Friedrich Gauss, Srinivasa Ramanujam, etc., were expert mathematicians even when they were still in their teens. Sri Sri Ravishankar of Art of Living, a great humanitarian and a towering spiritual leader of our era, used to recite the entire Bhagavad-Gita when he was just about 4 years old. There are innumerous examples of such child prodigies.

In the normal life, we know that if someone has to gain knowledge and proficiency in any chosen field, say a language or an art then one has to undergo several years of training to learn it. Even to learn a simple skill like driving an automobile, one has to undergo several days of training and several days of practicing. Thus, it is logical to conclude that without learning and practicing we know that no other magic is possible. But if somebody is displaying not just ordinary inclination but masterful craft at a very tender and unbelievable age, we are unable to come up with an appropriate logical explanation. The Prarabdha Karma (PK) identified by the Vedic philosophy seems to provide the only acceptable explanation which is that the skill has been acquired in the past life (or lives) and is getting exhibited at an early age in this birth.

There are various examples of how people enduring not so favorable PK, still managed to face it boldly and achieved great heights. Beethoven had become almost completely deaf when he composed his greatest music "Symphony No. 9". Helen Keller is a remarkably shining example of hope, achievement and determination as she achieved incredible heights after losing both her sight and hearing around the age of 2 years. She wrote several articles, was a prolific author, prominent political and social activist, world-renowned speaker and winner of American Presidential Medal of Freedom in 1964. Thanks to Helen Keller's work, Braille became the standard system around the world.

PK determines the experiences one has to undergo starting right from the birth until the end of one's life. Accepting the theory of PK brings meaning to the act of doing good deeds and refraining from indulging in harmful actions because according to PK we have to experience the results of our deeds. Though the phenomenon of past and future births cannot be proven with authority, if not anything, the theory of PK promotes doing good, harmonious living, peaceful coexistence and paves the way for a better civilized world because the belief in PK forces us to uphold the Golden Rule *"Do unto others as you would have them do unto you"*.

The main purpose of understanding PK is to become aware of our own strengths and weaknesses. In a class full of students, though the teaching is the same, it is received and understood differently by each student according to their abilities. Each person is born with his or her own unique capabilities, they differ from person to person and Vedas call this as Prarabdha Karma.

It augurs well to remember Stephen Hawking's words *"there is always something every one of us can do and succeed at"*. We need to identify the strength we are born with which comes naturally to us and use it well to our advantage.

Doing Svadhyaya (self-study) on PK enables us to understand our own capabilities and limitations, gracefully accept the strengths and humbly accept the limitations without any worries which is the main thing and wisely choose a profession that makes use of the best capabilities we possess. In case our efficiency is not adequate then we need to take steps to enhance our knowledge and skills to overcome our shortcomings such as taking additional training, reading books, watching videos, seeking help from the experts in the domain, etc.

Vasanas (VA)

The word **Vasanas** (VA) does not have an exact translation in English. Vasanas can be described as unmanifested desires, inherent traits and latent tendencies a person is born with. Just like the habits whether good or bad that we form in our current birth and find it difficult to quit them, the Vasanas are the channels carved by our habitual ways and long-lasting imprints that we have been carrying since several of our past lives. Vasanas strongly influence one's personality as they cause intense desires, disquietude, cloud the clarity of thoughts and sometimes strong Vasanas cause one to act with haste and impetuousness. Imprints from painful experiences create Vasanas of dislike, fear and phobia.

According to Swami Sivananda, founder of Divine Life Society, Vasana is a wave in the mind-lake. Just like plants are latent in the seeds and sprout when the time and environment are conducive, the Vasanas remain latent in the seed form seated in the Karana Sharira (Causal Body) and manifest in the mind-lake during favorable conditions. Vasanas blossom out like flowers one by one, come to the surface of the mind causing restless agitations, generate Sankalpas (desire to act) and goad a person to strive to possess and enjoy that particular object of enjoyment to satisfy the craving of that Vasana. Vasanas cause actions and actions in turn, strengthen the Vasanas making it a vicious circle and cause a person to engage in desire gratifications repeatedly. The actions add to the karma and one is bound to experience their results.

There are three types of Vasanas. **Deha Vasana** (bodily desires), **Shastra Vasana** (knowledge desires) and **Loka Vasana** (worldly desires).

- **Deha Vasana** causes irresistible cravings for food, sexual urges and fantasies, habits, vices, etc. There are also positive Vasanas such as liking to exercise, dance, music, sports and other activities related to the use of the body and kinesthetic skills.

- **Shastra Vasana** is the natural liking towards a particular topic or subject such as mathematics, science, literature, psychology, study of scriptures, etc. The topic of interest could also be harmful and destructive like interest in robbery, looting, bomb making, arson, sabotage, etc.

- **Loka Vasana** is the desire for name, fame, power, property, liking to live in a particular kind of environment, desire to visit specific type of places, etc.

Ramana Maharshi distinguishes between good and bad Vasanas. Good Vasanas like generosity, intimacy with parents, respect for elders, quest for knowledge, compassion, love, devotion to God, etc. do not cause harm. Bad Vasanas which go against the nature and civilized behavior do.

Vasanas cause restlessness, bondage and accumulate karma through the actions. Vasanas can be destroyed by discrimination and taking the necessary corrective steps with determination.

Environment (EN)

The **Environment** (EN) in which a child is born plays a prominent role in the development of its personality and lays the foundation for its belief system, habits, values, attitudes and behavioral inclinations. Here, the environment includes parents, grandparents, siblings, relatives, friends, neighborhood, community, religion, customs, traditions, culture, politics, city, nation, etc. The child gets programmed based on the stimuli and input received from the environment and builds its "**Samskara**" which is the culture that gets ingrained. Each child gets influenced uniquely as the environment differs from religion to religion, region to region, country to country, east to west, north to south, different costumes, different languages, varied food styles and in many more ways.

Parents are responsible for promoting and supporting the physical, emotional, social and intellectual development of a child from infancy to adulthood. The role of parents in influencing the development of the personality of a child cannot be emphasized enough. *"Good parenting helps foster empathy, honesty, self-reliance, self-control, kindness, cooperation and cheerfulness"*, says American child psychology expert Laurence Steinberg.

As parents, we need to be happy, cheerful, live and conduct ourselves first the way we expect from our children. Whenever our children talk to us, we need to give them our undivided attention by putting aside the newspaper, TV, gadgets, etc. We should have regular meals together as a family and celebrate together as often as we can. We need to teach our children to manage their emotions, think positively, build meaningful relationships, develop generosity, forgiveness, respect for elders and enjoy being of service to others. Strict discipline should be enforced regarding the amount of time our children spend with TV, smartphone, digital tablets and other devices. Too much love never spoils children. Children become spoiled when we substitute *'presents'* for *'presence'* says Dr. Anthony P. Witham.

It is observed that from infancy to the early teens, parents can effectively influence in molding a child's character and personality. Right from the time the child is expected, parents could discuss, plan and decide on each one deliberately introducing a few different valuable habits into the child. Reading is one of the most important habits that could be one of the greatest gifts a child could receive.

Start from reading bedtime stories without fail such as Cinderella, Rapunzel, Pocahontas, Winnie the Pooh, Little Red Riding Hood, etc. Children should always be kissed goodnight even if they are already asleep. As the child grows up, we could together do the reading of various Amar Chitra Katha comic books, Jataka Tales, Panchatantra Stories, etc. and cover as much of the evergreen children's classics written by great authors like Dr. Seuss, Lewis Carroll, Beatrix Potter, Louisa May Alcott, R.L. Stevenson, Rudyard Kipling, A.A. Milne, H.G. Wells, Jules Verne, etc. These efforts would eventually make the child capable of reading and enjoying on its own and move onto varied all-time celebrated authors such as Shakespeare, Charles Dickens, Thomas Hardy, George Bernard Shaw, Leo Tolstoy,

R.K. Narayan, Rabindranath Tagore, Mark Twain, Ernest Hemingway, Ralph Emerson, etc.

Children should be exposed to as many activities, games and sports as possible. Discipline, coaxing and cajoling could be employed if required, to forcibly introduce the child into level-1 courses of as many activities as possible. Activities could be chess, painting, music, dance, computer programming, public speaking, swimming, skating, yoga, table tennis, lawn tennis, badminton, basketball, etc. Let the introduction to an activity be enforced. But the further continuation of the activity can be based on the child's interest. Outdoor exploration should be encouraged as part of the family picnic or as part of a group tour with other children. At a young age itself, we should make efforts to leave the child to stay for a few days away from parents and home in a safe and trusted environment by enrolling them into various child development programs offered by reputed and credible institutions.

When the child is about to enter the teens, we should develop the comfort of talking without inhibition about anything with the child as appropriate such as procreation, opposite sex, infatuation, addiction, drugs, vices, human behaviors, politics, history, sports, etc. Father is considered as a role model by the children and as the child approaches the teens, one should start treating the child as an adult and a friend. We should freely discuss the day-to-day challenges faced, for example in the profession, the possible solutions and finally how it worked out at the end. Children love being respected as adults and discussing about our own profession helps build their self-confidence, broadens their knowledge and strengthens the bondage.

It is quite normal in a family to have difference of opinions between parents. Parents should never quarrel openly in front of their children and in case an issue needs to be sorted out, it is better to go out and find a secluded place or have a walk in the park, talk it over and settle the issue one way or the other. It is important for the parents to openly express mutual respect and love, often hug each other or hug the entire family and even go ahead and have a playful pillow fight involving the entire family.

We have delved into the importance of parenting so much as parents are just not only responsible for the upbringing of the children but also play a major role in shaping of the very personality of the child.

There are some interesting examples of how the Environment has played a vital role in shaping the lives of some personalities.

We already saw how the teachers of the hyperactive kid, Thomas Alva Edison found it difficult to handle him while describing the section on Ghatana (incident). His mother Nancy, took him out of school and taught him at home. She encouraged him with his experiments and allowed him to work at his early age and did not mind him coming home late even though he was still in his teens. Because of the foundation he got from his mother's efforts, Edison went on to become America's one of the most prolific inventors. Later in life, Edison said, *"My mother was the making of me. She was so true, so sure of me: and I felt I had something to live for, someone I must not disappoint"*.

A renowned novelist in Kannada language, T. R. Subba Rao, popularly known as TaRaSu, in his magnum opus "Durgasthamana" (sunset of Chitradurga) beautifully narrates a hair-raising incident about the King Madakari Nayaka. Madakari lived in the 18th century, ruled Chitradurga, was known for his bravery and shrewd administration. Chitradurga is now a district in the South Indian State, Karnataka. Before his coronation as a king, Madakari was given all-round training including the battle skills. All the training was arranged and keenly overseen by his Grandmother. One evening, the young Madakari after a rigorous physical training session, sweating profusely comes to the washroom where he meets his Grandmother who was waiting for him to talk about something important. As she waits near the entrance, Madakari enters the bathroom, using the water stored in a vessel, starts washing his face. He finds that he is not able to feel fresh and clean. He pours more water from the vessel and tries to wash his face again. Strangely he feels much more sticky and dirty. As the bathroom was not well lit, with the vessel in one hand, he comes out of the washroom into the twilight to examine. To his horror, he finds that his hand is completely red dripping with blood. He looks into the vessel and finds that it actually contains blood instead of water. He raises his head and throws a questioning look at his Grandmother. His Grandmother sternly without any facial expression tells him that as he is going to become a king soon, he is being trained to become a fearless warrior by developing the attitude of being as much at ease with the sight of blood as he is with water. Madakari went on to become a valiant king and a lionhearted warrior and even today is cherished as an icon in the heritage of Karnataka.

Children are not just influenced by parents but also by all other elders around them. So, it is important for us to spend some good time with the children of our relatives, friends and for that matter any child with whom we interact.

Education (ED)

The **Education** (ED) received by every child is unique and plays a dominant role irrespective of the gender in influencing one's character and personality. Education inculcates the habit of learning, enables the acquisition of knowledge, develops intelligence, skills, values, beliefs and causes personal advancement. Education is a most powerful tool as it enables the child to build up its confidence, teaches to think intensively and critically, collect facts, evidence and references, question everything to make better and informed decisions and makes one strong mentally, socially and intellectually.

A sound education should bring transformation in one's life, provide the courage to stand up against blind beliefs and discriminating customs, understand the realities of life and should empower the people to live happily as well as radiate happiness all around. Otherwise, the education loses its meaning if it does not promote peace, harmony, tolerance and universal brotherhood.

In the modern era, education is a must to secure a job of one's choice, pursue better prospects and succeed in life. To emphasize this, the former first lady of the USA, Michelle Obama, says, *"You have to stay in school. You have to go to college. You have to get your degree. Because that's the one thing people can't take away from you. And it is worth the investment".*

A library is a temple of learning and it is desirable if one is encouraged to strengthen the habit of making use of the library right from the school stage, continue it to the college level and should become an established habit as one enters the professional career.

It tremendously helps to become a successful professional if one "always has a current book" that is being read. The reading can happen at one's own comfortable pace and once the book is completed another book can take its place and become the current book. Nowadays it is a tragedy to see that many professionals with years of experience have not read or purchased a book ever since they graduated from the college. People seem to rely more on blogs and the Internet which is not bad as the blog may provide valuable information but would not cover a topic from end to end. But a book written by a subject matter expert would cover the topic thoroughly, provide highly useful insights, tips and guidance. The author with the experience and expertise would also be sharing masterful skills, secrets of the trade and articulate on certain nuances of the subject that might border artistry.

The teachers have a tremendous responsibility towards teaching the children to develop love and passion for learning, igniting the intelligence, instilling hope and confidence, inspiring creativity and imagination, kindling the curiosity to explore, invent and discover and awaken the joy in widening the knowledge.

Bill Gates in his blog post, "A Teacher Who Changed My Life", reminisces how Mrs. Caffiere, the librarian at Seattle's View Ridge Elementary enabled Gates, a timid, shy and nerdy nine-year-old fourth grader to emerge out of his shell, encouraged and stoked his love for books. Gates fondly remembers how Mrs. Caffiere helped spark his interest and instilled confidence which is currently making him do his bit in helping children get the benefit of great teachers. He concludes by saying,

"It's remarkable how much power one good person can have in shaping the life of a child".

Emily Blunt, the British actress, a Golden Globe award winner, disclosed that at the age of 12 she turned mute as she was so anguished at having a stutter. She says that her parents tried everything from consulting various specialists to different treatments, but all those efforts failed to help. One of her caring teachers nudged and pepped her to take part in a school play talking with a funny voice and accent. It did the trick in bolstering her confidence and finally overcome her stuttering problem. She went on to become a celebrated actress.

Learning need not always happen from a teacher in a school or college. Anyone around us is capable of providing valuable learning provided we are ever ready to receive the education. In the corporate world, it is common to have a "Mentorship Program" where a group of juniors picks up a prototype project and a senior colleague is expected to guide them to realize the prototype. Though this is good, it would be better if the mentorship frequently happens on the regular job itself.

A senior professional, instead of just asking about the status from a junior, should be willing to sit with the junior colleague, understand the problem he or she is struggling with and should demonstrate by example the efficient approach that can be adopted to nail the issue at hand. Similarly, an aspiring junior should not sit around and wait for some expert colleague to come by and do the handholding. Instead, a junior has the responsibility to start developing the expertise by digging into the several works already done by the senior colleagues, understanding and learning from them and developing an eye to admire the masterful craftsmanship and the pieces of beautiful artistry and finesse that might lie hidden in those works.

Education is not just an academic qualification but it is the knowledge and wisdom gained. Failing to put the learnt knowledge into proper application and effective execution would render the knowledge bookish, theoretical and almost useless. It is not at all uncommon to see people in highly responsible positions, lacking in comprehensive understanding of the fundamentals of their profession. They have a degree from a good school, talk effectively during the interview making heavy use of technical jargons, but miserably fail when it comes to deliverables, meeting deadlines, rendering production quality work and cause maintenance nightmares.

Probably before every promotion, conducting a "Seniority cum Suitability" test may be called for to ensure that the employees at all levels are firmly grounded in the fundamentals, essential skills and the ethics needed by the profession. This would ensure that the importance is not given just to the academic knowledge and years of experience, but also for the execution skills and does not make the promotions automatic based only on the seniority. It also allows enthusiastic and knowledgeable youngsters to exhibit their skills and talent, climb up the ladder quickly and occupy higher and more responsible positions if they are found deserving. This could effectively prevent arrogance and complacency setting in and discourage lackadaisical attitudes.

Education should never stop, learning should never end and one should be an earnest student throughout the life. If one develops a voracious appetite for learning, then growth would never cease and success is bound to arrive.

Experience (EX)

Experience (EX) is an invaluable education the "school of life" has to offer and the teachings received are all-important as they come directly from the reality of interacting with the world around us. Our experiences shape and alter our thought process, mindset, attitude, social behaviors, response to situations, circumstances and events. Strength, courage and confidence are gained by every experience and empower us to face any fear, challenge or adversity confidently.

Einstein says, *"The only source of knowledge is experience"*. Indeed, there are some legendary stories where the Einstein's words come alive verbatim. The most famous one is the experience of Isaac Newton observing the fall of an apple from a tree in an orchard. Just that experience inspired him to discover the laws of gravity. A simple day-to-day experience of water overflowing the bathtub when one lowers the body into it sparked Archimedes to understand the laws of buoyancy, thrilled with his discovery he ecstatically exclaimed "Eureka".

In the professional work environment, the senior professionals have a great responsibility towards providing valuable experience to the juniors. The flair for knowledge, skillful craftsmanship, eyeing elegant, yet simple solutions, artistic way of expressing all of them in work, etc., might have been learnt and acquired over several years of experience. But if the will is there then that valuable knowledge acquired over several years could be shared as part of the regular working with the aspiring junior colleagues in a matter of months or days. To facilitate this free sharing of knowledge, juniors should be required to share in their yearly feedback about their senior colleagues, at least three or more technical skills / ideas / insights that they have learnt from each senior colleague, which have helped them to work smartly, efficiently and enabled them to make significant contributions.

Everybody's experience is unique. Nothing can substitute the direct realization obtained from one's own experience. It is important to stay alert, keep our eyes and ears wide open so that we do not let a beautiful and important experience fly by unnoticed. Failures need not be feared as they are bound to happen. But every failure can be used as a stepping stone to success. Helen Keller says, *"Character cannot be developed in ease and quiet. Only through experience of trial and suffering can the soul be strengthened, ambition inspired and success achieved"*.

Personality Summary

The personality of every individual is influenced by Prarabdha Karma (PK), Vasanas (VA), Environment (EN), Education (ED) and Experience (EX). Each one is unique for every individual and their combination also becomes unique and that's why different people have different personalities.

A unique insight into this reveals that there is an interplay between Environment, Education and Experience. Whatever we might have learnt and adopted in one, might get altered by what we learn from another. To illustrate the point let us take a simple and silly example. A mother while feeding a toddler, to make the child eat, might induce fear saying a ghost would come or a policeman might show up if the food is not eaten. Though the child might believe it to be true at that age, as it grows up, the child would understand it to be not true. Thus, several of the beliefs, customs, behaviors and thinking that the child might absorb from Environment might get changed because of Education as the child gains more knowledge and discrimination. Similarly, several ideals learnt in Education might get changed due to Experience as the touch of reality kicks in. In the same way, the knowledge gained and the opinions formed due to Experience might get changed due to the newer inputs coming from Environment or Education.

"Whatever is impressed is expressed", says Aristotle. It is important to develop an all-around, pleasant, confident and enthusiastic personality. We should also be aware that as a parent, relative, colleague, friend and fellow citizen we are in a position to influence the personalities of others and hence it is imperative on every one of us to be aware of this responsibility we carry and discharge it responsibly.

Ego

"ego" is the only requirement to destroy any relationship. So, be a bigger person skip the "e" and let it "go"!

– Evan Carmichael

Ego is an illusory false identity which we construct based on our personality, capability, talent, education, skills, wealth, status, power, etc. Though the ego is artificial, inaccurate and a false identity, it wields a powerful influence on our thoughts, feelings, emotions and behavior. The ego strongly manifests as I, me and mine. If the ego is not kept under control, it fuels negative tendencies such as expecting to always exercise control over the people around, judging and criticizing others, insisting that always one's views and opinions should prevail, being constantly in need of approval and appreciation, trying to feel special and superior, etc. Eventually, the ego becomes the cause for fear, anxiety, worry, suffering and despair.

The same thing is conveyed in another way by the ancient Vedic texts where it is said that Ego (ahamkara) is built and shaped by one's personality which consists of Manas (mind), Buddhi (intellect) and Chitta (memory).

- The ability of the Manas (mind) to grasp, interpret and react gives rise to the feeling "I am smart", "I possess these talents", "My skills are exceptional", etc.

- The wisdom of the Buddhi (intellect) makes one feel "My education is the best", "I have read these many books and scriptures", "My knowledge is vast", etc.

- The Chitta (memory) makes one think "My experience is wide", "I have found solutions to many complex problems", "I can easily face any new challenges", etc.

All these three together conspire to prop up the fictional ego emboldening one to hurt someone or in the process get hurt.

Sigmund Freud says that there are three components that make up a human personality, viz., id, ego and superego.

- "Id" is part of the unconscious mind, is the most basic part of the personality, full of instincts without any regard to whether they are moral or logical and fuels the needs, wants, desires, passions and impulses.

- "Ego" acts based on the reality principle, always tries to satisfy the drives and desires of "id" in a way that is acceptable to the social world we live in. If it feels that it can get away without being caught, "ego" does not hesitate to fulfill the needs of "id" even if they are illogical and immoral.

- "Superego" is the inner conscience or the inner voice that acts as a fatherly figure, dispassionately judges what is right and wrong and always suggests to "ego" what is logically correct and morally right.

According to Freud, "ego" though biased towards "id" and always trying to please it, does so by trying to strike a balance between "id", "superego" and the external world.

Sri Ramana Maharshi says that ego is like a ghost; in reality, it does not exist and is nothing but a trick played by the mind. Though at first glance it appears contradictory to what Freud says, it is actually not so. In Ramana's wisdom, he is advising us to practice calmness and patience. With a still and serene mind, if one tries to go inwards and critically takes a look at the ego, he says that the ego takes flight along with its illogical, insatiable passions and desires.

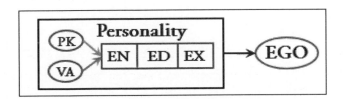

When a child is born, it does not have an ego or its ego is said to be in a dormant state. As the child grows, ego develops and is continuously altered and shaped by getting influenced by all the components of the personality described in the earlier section, which are Prarabdha Karma (PK), Vasanas (VA), Environment (EN), Education (ED) and Experience (EX).

- Due to Prarabdha Karma (PK), if one is born beautiful or strong or smart, it could give rise to the ego. It should be noted that it is the same ego responsible for negative thoughts and depression such as "I am not that beautiful" or "I am not that tall", etc.

- Due to Vasanas (VA), one might feel proud of one's likes, dislikes, habits, etc. and display an ego.

- If one is born to wealthy parents or a powerful politician, that Environment (EN) might develop an ego due to the social status.

- Getting Education (ED) by studying in a reputed school, obtaining higher grades, etc., could cause the ego to bloat up.

- A person who had an expensive dinner or stayed in a luxurious resort might boast about that Experience (EX) in almost every other sentence during a conversation.

Alternatively, the knowledge gained from Environment, Education and Experience could also result in tempering of the ego if one puts the knowledge to good use and develops discrimination, humility, love and compassion.

The reality we perceive and experience in the physical world is actually a reflection of what we feel and think inside our mind. According to Ramana Maharshi, *"All bad qualities center around the ego. When the ego is gone, Realization results by itself"*.

According to Vedanta, we all are the **Sentient Life Energy**, Awareness, Consciousness, Self or Atman. It is this energy which is providing us the life every moment and powers all the body organs such as heart, lungs, eyes, ears, hands, legs, etc. This life energy is sentient, which means this energy, Atman has the ability to know, ability to become aware or the ability to become conscious. In other words, Atman is the Knower, Perceiver, Awareness, Consciousness or Sentience. Vedanta says that the real "I" is this Atman, the Self. Instead, we wrongly identify "I" with the ego which is the lower self. Thus, the ego acts as a veil and hides the real Self.

Kanaka Dasa, a great devotee, philosopher and a Kannada language poet who lived during late sixteenth century said that dropping the ego, getting rid of I, me and mine reveals the real Self, the Atman, the Chit Shakti, the **Sentient Life Energy**. Wikipedia article on Kanaka Dasa registers his proclamation as *"If 'I' goes away, then 'going' will happen"* which means *"Give up ego to get going"*. Vedic texts show us the ways and means to effectively drop the ego which we shall study in detail in the subsequent chapters.

Arishadvarga - Passions of the Mind

"He who reigns within himself and rules passions, desires and fears is more than a king."

– John Milton

Ari means enemy. Shad means six. Varga means a band or a group. Arishadvarga means a band of six enemies capable of wreaking havoc in the life of a human being. Arishadvarga is mentioned in the Maitreya Upanishad (3.18) and Varaha Upanishad (1.10). The six powerful factors or passions constantly influencing the mind are **KA**ma (Desire, Lust), **KR**odha (Anger), **LO**bha (Miserliness, Greed), **MO**ha (Extreme Obsession, Delusory Emotional Attachment), **MA**da (Pride, Vanity and Arrogance) and **MaT**sarya (Envy, Jealousy).

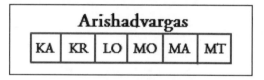

The Bible also warns about seven deadly or cardinal sins which are similar to Arishadvarga. They are pride, avarice (greed), lust, envy, gluttony (excessive eating), wrath (anger) and sloth (sluggishness or laziness).

Arishadvarga, the set of six enemies spread their tentacles to entrap the mind and hold it under their sway. They act like glasses of color shades and distort the comprehension of the mind and do not allow the mind to see clearly and impartially as things are. As John Milton says, we need to reign over these passions, otherwise, we would be allowing them to reign over our mind dragging us into a quagmire of fear, anxiety, anger, pain and suffering. These passions derive their power from an inflated ego. Hence it becomes important to use the valuable knowledge gained from Environment, Education and Experience to develop reasoning, discrimination and prudence to bring the ego under control and overcome the obstacles placed by the Providence in the form of Arishadvarga.

Kama - Desire

Kama (KA) means the desire which is very much desirable if it manifests as aspiration, ambition, undeterred determination, appetite for knowledge, relentless effort to make progress, eagerness to venture, motivation to relish the success, zeal to achieve, fervor to endeavor, yearning to reach a goal, etc. Without such kind of positive desires which are useful to an individual as well as to the society, there is no meaning and purpose to life.

Desires become problematic if they make a person extremely self-indulgent in all kinds of sensual and materialistic pleasures such as wealth, property, honor, status, fame, indulgence in luxury and craving for instant gratifications. Such desires are like the paper tissues packed in a box. Pull out one tissue, another is raised up automatically to be pulled out. Trying to control such desires by satisfying them is like trying to douse a fire using gasoline. Intense desire leads to lust making a person crazy and become restless to satisfy it at any cost. There is a Sanskrit saying, *"Kamaturanam na bhuya na lajja"*, meaning a person blinded by lust has neither fear nor shame.

As a desire becomes stronger and forces a person to engage in actions to satisfy it, there will be doubt and uncertainty until the desire is fulfilled, which results in the sense of fear and anxiety to creep in. Even after the objective is achieved, say the possession of a property or acquisition of some wealth, the fear and anxiety could continue as the desire now shifts to maintaining the possession safely and securely.

If the desire is not satisfied, it results in Krodha (anger). Krodha has this relationship with all other components of Arishadvarga as Krodha is the end result if the objective is not achieved.

Thus, we see that if not careful, one has to live in fear while pursuing a desire and sometimes even after the desire is satisfied the fear might continue if there is a responsibility of secrecy, safety and security. The other alternative is that one has to live with Krodha (anger) if the desire is not satisfied. Desire can toss us between fear and anger if we do not use prudence and lose our common sense.

If the desires are controlled, then all other components of Arishadvarga can be held under check. To warn us against the pain and suffering caused by the endless selfish desires, Buddha emphatically said, *"Desire is the root cause of all evil"*.

Krodha - Anger

Krodha (KR) means anger and is related to all other components of Arishadvarga. Krodha is the end result; if Kama (desire) is thwarted, Lobha (miserliness) is kindled by loss of a desired object, Moha (obsession) is not satisfied due to failure in attaining an object of obsession, Mada (pride) is hurt by someone's dismissive behavior or Matsarya (envy) is fueled due to someone else's success. Analyzing and knowing which of these are the cause for the anger helps reduce its intensity, dispel the delusion and allows the fresh breeze of sense and sanity to prevail.

If forced to swallow Krodha, it leads to brooding, loathing, sulking, grumpiness, worry, agony, grief, dejection and depression. If Krodha is not controlled, it could result in friction, hostility, aversion, revenge, vengeance, enmity, intolerance, hatred, etc.

The anger first has an effect internally such as increased heart rate, elevated blood pressure, fast and shallow breathing causing "constipation of thoughts and resulting in diarrhea of words".

The external expression of uncontrolled anger could cause harm, hurt, grief, damage long-lasting relationships and could even bring about severe self-destruction. *"Speak when you are angry and you'll make the best speech you'll ever regret"*, says Laurence J. Peter, well known for formulating the concept of "Peter Principle".

Lobha – Miserliness

Lobha (LO) means miserliness and it is an excessive selfish desire to cling on to something and not willing to part with even a fraction of it to others. Normally, Lobha is associated with the tendency to keep accumulating wealth along with extreme hesitation to spend even for essential needs. Lobha is also seen when someone refuses to share even excess food with the hungry, unwillingness to part with the knowledge and in general not caring to help anyone in need even if one is in a position to help without losing anything.

Lobha and Greed are two sides of the same coin. Lobha is an obsession to retain wealth whereas Greed is an obsession to acquire wealth. If Lobha is aroused by having to forcibly part with some of the possessions or Greed gets thwarted then it could result in Krodha (anger).

Glorious John Dryden, the British poet says, *"Go miser go, for money sell your soul. Trade wares for wares and trudge from pole to pole. So, others may say when you are dead and gone, see what a vast estate he left his son"*.

Moha – Obsession

Moha (MO) means obsession and it is a state of extreme Kama (desire), a delusory emotional attachment where one reaches a stage of attaining the desired object at any cost. If the desire is legit and can be satisfied, then there is nothing like Moha, for example loving somebody and succeeding in making the same person as the life partner.

Moha could become a source of trouble and misery if the desire is immoral, illegitimate or unachievable such as coveting someone else's property, lusting for someone else's spouse, craving to possess something that is not affordable, etc. Mahatma Gandhi says, *"The world has enough for everyone's need, but not enough for everyone's greed"*.

However, the obsession (Moha) to achieve, deliver high-quality work, attain perfection, provide customer satisfaction, etc., bring out one's creativity to the fore, push one's capabilities and limits to the hilt, and experience ecstasy when the desired goal is realized.

Mada-Pride

In Sanskrit, Garva exactly translates to pride. **Mada** (MA) more accurately refers to the incorrigible behavior of someone intoxicated due to an inflated ego, feeling very special and superior about oneself, goes on to disrespect and despise people around without any regard to elders, learned people, their status, etc.

Ancient Indian texts talk about Ashtamada (eight prides) which are Anna Mada (pride of food), Artha Mada (pride of wealth), Tarunya Mada (pride of youth), Sthree Mada (pride of women), Vidya Mada (pride of learning), Kula Mada (pride of rank and family), Rupa Mada (pride of beauty and physique) and Udyoga Mada (pride of professional position, power, contacts and influence).

There are certain cousins of Mada which are mentioned in the Bhagavad-Gita, 16th chapter, 4th verse. They are Dambha (hypocrisy, pomposity), Darpa (arrogance), Abhimana (false ego) and Paarushyam (harshness, rudeness).

If any of these prides is not respected, then it results in the outburst of anger. Regarding pride, Saint Augustine says, *"It was pride that changed angels into devils; it is humility that makes men as angels".*

Matsarya-Envy

Matsarya (MT) is the state of envy where one feels unhappy, discontented and miserable due to somebody else's happiness, wealth, status, abilities and rewards. The French poet Victor Hugo says, *"The wicked envy and hate; it is their way of admiring".*

Matsarya has two close siblings, Asuya and Irshya. **Asuya** is being jealous and intolerant of someone else's progress irrespective of whether that person is of the same status, much below or above us. Asuya is basically not liking anybody else's well-being other than our own. **Irshya** is the ill-feeling on seeing that another is not being subjected to the same sufferings as oneself.

Arishadvarga Summary

We need to be cautious of Arishadvarga, the six internal enemies that pollute the mind and every one of us is forced to deal with them. As already mentioned, if we control the first one which is the "Desire", we could control the rest. Developing simplicity, humility, forgiveness, love, compassion, reducing selfishness and ego do help in controlling the never-ending demands of the desires.

Let us say for some reason I am possessed by a strong desire to own and wear an exorbitantly expensive dress which I happened to see. I am convinced that I would be extremely happy and delighted if I could get that dress. Let us say now that exactly the same expensive dress is made available to me on one condition that I can wear that dress inside a closed room in my home with windows and doors closed and no one including the family members should get to see me. I can wear the dress any number of times and I am allowed to look at myself in the mirror and admire, but no one should be able to see me. Would I be happy wearing that dress and honoring the condition?

I cannot respect the condition because the dress is considered useless if nobody gets to see me wearing it. The rampaging desires of the mind immediately drop once the condition was put. That's because the mind with its agitating desires was conspiring to possess the dress, not because of true love for it but because by wearing it I wanted others to appreciate how stunning I look, wanted jaws to drop hearing the price and pamper my ego by showing off my vanity. By examining closely our own desires of the mind, the trickery of the mind gets exposed and the mind becomes very uncomfortable because it is not used to and does not like being very closely watched or observed. Actually, it is really not trickery of the mind but it is trickery of the wretched ego. It is because of the ego, the mind behaves that way and generates imaginary, fancy, self-centered thoughts.

The very process of observing the thoughts renders the thoughts powerless, the intensity of the desires weakens and the calm and serene silence is experienced. Ramana Maharshi emphasizes that enjoying the silent mind is our true nature which is our "being". He says the constant practice of this technique would make our mind quiet, our false ego would take flight, the desires would recede and the feelings of inadequacy would subside.

"Life is full of something less and something more". When something is there, we feel something more is required. When everything is there, we feel there is something less. While seeking for something, we miss many things. While looking for missing things, we miss something already present. Why can't we stop looking for something? We definitely can, if we realize that the desire for something more or the feeling of something less are just the tricks played by the mind due to the selfish ego. We just have to start learning to say "Enough" to be happy, satisfied and contented with what we have.

A sincere seeker has the ultimate goal of realizing the Truth. A devotee's goal irrespective of the religion is to reach the beloved God. A professional's goal is to succeed in the current project. A business person's goal is to succeed in the business. The Arishadvarga (band of six enemies) impedes one in succeeding in attaining the desired goal.

However, a deft person can make use of a unique insight to use these deadly Arishadvarga to one's advantage. We could harbor and nourish only those "desires" that move us closer towards the desired goal. We need to be "angry" with ourselves if we forget our goal sometimes and indulge in other activities that distract us from our goal. We need to be "miserly" in devoting our time, energy and resources towards anything that is unrelated to our goal. Let us be "obsessed" in reaching our goal with quality and perfection. Let us take "pride" in our sincere and stupendous efforts to succeed. Let us have a healthy "jealousy" with an undercurrent of admiration and respect when we come across sincere, talented, knowledgeable and dedicated fellow human beings who have advanced more in treading towards a goal similar to ours.

Pancha Klesha – Afflictions of the Mind

"Teach self-denial and make its practice pleasure, and you can create for the world a destiny more sublime that ever issued from the brain of the wildest dreamer."

– Sir Walter Scott

Pancha means five. Klesha means poison. Pancha Klesha means five poisons that afflict the mind and they are mentioned in the "Yoga Sutras" of Maharshi Patanjali. The five hindrances or obstacles that afflict the mind are **AV**idya (ignorance), **AS**mita (egoism), **RA**ga (attractions), **DW**esha (aversions) and **AB**hinivesha (fear of the unknown). These inherent defects combine with the Arishadvarga (band of six enemies) and the traits of our personality and strongly influence the mind.

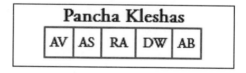

Pancha Kleshas				
AV	AS	RA	DW	AB

Avidya – Ignorance

Avidya (AV), ignorance, means lack of Vidya (knowledge). Generally, Avidya means illiteracy or lack of knowledge. According to Vedanta, Avidya means the ignorance of our true nature, the veil which needs to be removed so that the knowledge of our true nature could dawn which is calmness, peace, love and compassion. Avidya makes it difficult to separate the real from the unreal, makes us mistake impure for the pure and confuses us to consider something that could cause pain to be the source of pleasure.

Avidya is the mother of all kleshas and it immediately strengthens Asmita (egoism). Then Avidya and Asmita together empower all the other three remaining kleshas. According to the American civil rights activist Martin Luther King, *"Nothing in all the world is more dangerous than sincere ignorance and conscientious stupidity"*.

Asmita – Egoism

Asmita (AS) is an offshoot of Avidya and it more accurately means I-ness because of which we start overidentifying with I, me and mine. Asmita is internal whereas Ego is external. That means even if one outwardly wears a mask of humbleness, internally the feeling of I might reign supreme.

The feeling of superiority makes one blind, lose wisdom, act in haste, hurt people around and eventually would end up in the inflated ego getting bruised, resulting in pain, suffering and self-deprecating thoughts. British philosopher John Ruskin says, *"Pride is at the bottom of all great mistakes"*.

Raga – Attractions

Raga (RA) refers to the likes, attractions and attachments. Due to Avidya (ignorance) and Asmita (I-ness), we develop certain strong biases and start getting attracted towards what we tend to like. There may not be valid or logical reasons for our likes, and the likings need not be always moral and legitimate. Raga can delude and cloud the thinking so much so that one might pursue the likes even if they endanger one's own safety, health, and wealth, jeopardize the family wellbeing, stake name and reputation, and disturb peace causing unrest.

Raga is subtle and eventually gives rise to desires. As we have already seen, once the desires strengthen they force us to act to satisfy them. The 13th century Italian philosopher Saint Thomas Aquinas says, *"Three things are necessary for the salvation of man: to know what he ought to believe; to know what he ought to desire; and to know what he ought to do"*.

Dwesha – Aversions

Dwesha (DW) refers to the dislikes, aversions and hatred. Dwesha is something that we want to stay away from or love to get rid of. Aversions and hatred destroy the peace of mind. It is better to practice forgiveness than to harbor Dwesha. Raga and Dwesha are two sides of the same coin. According to Socrates, *"From the deepest desires often come the deadliest hate"*.

Abhinivesha – Fear of the Unknown

Abhinivesha (AB) is the fear of the unknown. Most common greatest fear is the fear of death since what happens after death is unknown to us. Most of the times the thought of fear can be much greater than the actual fear itself. Most of the things which we fear might never happen or even if they do they may not be as bad as we feared.

Though we all know that in this world change is constant, there is a tendency to be always in the comfort zone fearing change. We need to be aware that too many irrational fears can make a permanent nest resulting in permanent stress.

If we succeed in dropping the ego, identify ourselves with the **Sentient Life Energy** and enjoy being in the **Silent Awareness** then we become fearless. Vivekananda says, *"If there is one word that you find coming out like a bomb from the Upanishads bursting like a bombshell upon masses of ignorance, it is the word 'Fearlessness', and the only religion that ought to be taught is the religion of fearlessness".*

Pancha Klesha Summary

Avidya (ignorance) is the root of all other kleshas. Once the ignorance is gone, the restless agitations of the mind stop, desires cease, selfishness ends, misery vanishes and the unruly behavior disappears, giving way to radiate happiness, love and compassion.

Asmita (I-ness) gets powered by Avidya (ignorance) and both together give rise to Raga (likes) and Dwesha (dislikes). When one strongly identifies with I, me and mine there is always Abhinivesha (fear of the unknown), which is always being concerned and fearing that the current comfort could be disturbed.

In a work environment also all these five afflictions can be counterproductive if not taken care of. A person in a senior and responsible position needs to have good knowledge in the field of profession.

We touched upon this subject while deliberating on the topic "Education". We are not talking about some expert knowledge, but a sound grasp of essential fundamentals that are demanded by the position held in the organization.

Due to nepotism, favoritism, coincidence or for some other reason, let us say a person with Avidya (ignorance) and not having the requisite knowledge and skills happens to lead a team. Naturally, such a person would not be able to "command" respect due to the lack of adequate knowledge and hence would start to "demand" respect by making use of the authority. Thus, the Asmita (I-ness) starts gaining strength. This, in turn, fuels strong currents of Raga (likes) and Dwesha (dislikes). People who get favored are those who are similar in nature, who may not be at the top of their professional skills, who flatter the leader who is in constant need of satisfying narcissistic demands, agree to everything the leader says and who do not question the authority of the leader. A large number of inefficient people get hired instead of a talented few. Meritocracy and talent take a back seat, creativity and innovation get stifled and the environment becomes smothering for the capable and efficient people.

Just as the saying goes "success breeds success", in this case, "inefficiency breeds inefficiency". With a bunch of inefficient people at the helm, the capable people becoming mute and made to sulk or quit, naturally the quality and the productivity become the casualty. After missing several deadlines, finally, the time arrives to make the delivery and reach the customer with the "hope" that it works. Customers get satisfied only if the delivery is made with confidence and not with hope. Inevitably Abhinivesha (fear) sets in as the troubles could start coming from all fronts as the quality of the delivery is not up to the mark. Eventually such kind of loss-making units abandon the projects after spending the significant amount of time and money, and in certain circumstances could lead to mass layoffs.

Time and again we see this phenomenon in large organizations. That's why most of the time innovation happens in startups where high risks are taken by the investors, which automatically leads to responsibility associated with accountability, resulting in the business and professional interests being given paramount importance. There is no place for Avidya or incompetence, nepotism and favoritism. Everybody is expected to pull their weight for the salary received, people are highly motivated by the creative work involved, let their work speak rather than the tongue, inspired by the joy of tasting the success and propelled by the opportunity of enjoying the results once the goal is achieved.

Sometimes the leader may be efficient and brilliant. But due to momentary Avidya (ignorance), a wrong decision may be taken or may fail to make the right decision. Unfortunately, sometimes such momentary indiscretions might prove to be a very costly mistake. Smartphone leader Nokia failed to notice the change in the consumer demands for Touchphone created by Apple. This Avidya (ignorance) lead to Asmita (I-ness) and hence loved their own Symbian platform so much, they failed to realize that it is reaching its expiry date. Yahoo made a blunder by not recognizing the value of the Search Engine when Google founders had offered to sell their idea for just $1 million. The Avidya (ignorance) about the power of the Search Engine algorithm that was on offer lead to Asmita (I-ness) which induced a touch of arrogance in thinking that being at the helm of as big as Yahoo one can do no wrong and thereby ended up committing a suicidal Himalayan Blunder. Novell Netware reached their peak and threw it all away. Borland International squandered their opportunities and plummeted further when they paid a hefty price to acquire Ashton-Tate which had already passed its prime. There are many such examples where lack of application of right knowledge has proved to be costly.

Knowledge is the key. Knowledge is power whether it is for the spiritual seeker or to be a successful professional. Knowledge removes Avidya (ignorance), and makes one humble, thereby reducing Asmita (I-ness), which in turn keeps all other kleshas (poisons) under check.

Outer World

"We can never obtain peace in the outer world until we make peace with ourselves"

– Dalai Lama

The outer world is the vast physical world comprising of our planet earth which in turn is part of the entire universe. The input and stimuli provided by the outer world contribute to the modifications of our inner world.

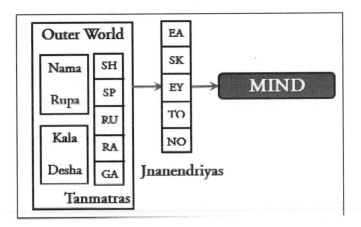

We interact with the world using our Jnanendriyas (the five sense organs). The objects perceived by the five senses are the five **Tanmatras** (subtle elements). We also cognize the outer world using **Nama** (name), **Rupa** (form), **Kala** (time) and **Desha** (place).

Tanmatras – Subtle Elements

Tan means subtle, matras means elements. Tanmatras means subtle elements. There are five Tanmatras, **SH**abdha (sound), **SP**arsha (touch), **Ru**pa (form), **Ra**sa (taste) and **GA**ndha (smell). Another meaning of Tan is mother and matra means matter – the mother of matter. The mother of this whole physical world is Tanmatras.

The Tanmatras are the objects of the five senses which are hearing, tactile perception, vision, taste and smell. We perceive these five senses using our five sense organs called Jnanendriyas (organs of knowledge). Jnana means knowledge and indriya means organ. The five Jnanendriyas are EAr (srotra), SKin (tvak), EYes (chakshu), TOngue (rasana) and NOse (ghrana).

The materials that facilitate the grasping of the five senses respectively are Aakash (ether or space), Vayu (air), Agni (fire), Jala (water) and Prithvi (earth). These five gross elements are called Pancha Bhootas (five elements). The Vedic literature says that this entire physical world is the manifestation of Pancha Bhootas. Our physical body is also made up of Pancha Bhootas (Garbha Upanishad) and once our life is over, the body merges back into the same Pancha Bhootas.

A mud pot was once asked, "How do you remain cool at all times?" The pot replied humbly, "I remind myself that I am made of mud and will return back to mud. Then why have pride and anger?"

We have exactly five sense organs to grasp the five Tanmatras and receive the stimuli and information from the physical world. The mind interprets the input received from the sense organs. We interact with the physical world using our five Karmendriyas (organs of action). Karma means action, indriya means organ. The five Karmendriyas are Vak (speech), Paani (hands), Paadha (feet), Paayu (excretory organ) and Upastha (organ of reproduction).

Nama – (Name)

Nama (name) is cognized by the mind and if it signifies a physical object, invariably the mind makes a mental image of the **Rupa** (form) of the object. That's why Nama and Rupa always go together. We name everything in this universe so that our mind can understand using that name. The name helps us even understand about things that do not have any form, such as evaporation, electricity, love, anger, profit, loss, near, far, heat, cold, etc.

Consider some names like Smith or Patel. We just recognize them as some names of people. Now consider the names Mary, Jesus, Pope, Allah, Mohammad and Krishna. Suddenly we do not consider these names as ordinary as in the previous example and unconsciously they automatically create a certain amount of importance and we experience passions and emotions.

We attach utmost importance to our own names as our name is considered as our identity. In a congregation, we rejoice when our name is called out for some recognition. If the ever attention craving ego were to have its ways, one would want the name to be inscribed everywhere, as the name of a street, name of a roundabout, name of a building, etc.

It is common to see that one attaches so much importance to one's name, but are we really the name? Would we be any different if we were to be called by any other name? Didn't our friends in school call us by different names like Johnny or Joe? Didn't parents call us differently to express their love by calling Sweetie Pie, Sugar Candy, etc.? Wouldn't the spouse call names like Honey, Sweet Heart, etc.? Using legal process also we could change our name. So, does changing the name change us as well? Do we lose our existence by changing our name? No!!

In Shakespeare's "Romeo and Juliet", there is a popular quote, *"A rose by any other name would smell as sweet"*. This captures the essence of the previous paragraph, brings forth the truth that there need not be any undue importance given to one's name and understand the fact that the purpose of a name is just to comprehend, transact and communicate.

Rupa – (Form)

Rupa (form) is associated with every physical object and as mentioned earlier, Nama and Rupa, the name and form go together. Nama and Rupa represent the mind and the body. Through the mind, we identify ourselves using the Nama. Similarly, we identify ourselves using our body and its Rupa (form).

We have already seen that the physical world is made of Pancha Bhootas (five gross elements) which are the gross manifestation of the five Tanmatras (subtle elements). The body is also made of the same Pancha Bhootas. Just like a rock, mud or metal is inert, the body is also inert or insentient. For example, when we look at our hand, it is not the hand that is looking at us, rather it is we who are looking at the hand. That is because the hand is inert or insentient. But we clearly feel that we are sentient and full of life energy. Hence, we cannot be the body, sentient cannot be the same as insentient. Nama is just a label given to the body. The realization that we are not mere name and form, instead, we are the energy which is nameless and formless is the goal of the Vedantic Philosophy.

In reality, we are influenced by the Rupa. We admire, get attracted when we see some form we like and we also get scared and sometimes even feel disgusted when we see some forms which we dislike.

Scientific research also acknowledges this and calls it as "Beauty Bias" which makes one think that the most handsome individual is also most smart and would be successful, forgetting that *"Beauty is only skin deep"*. For example, while 60% of CEOs in the US are over 6 feet, only 15% of the total population is over 6 feet tall. While 36% of US CEOs are over 6.2 feet, only 4% of the US population is over 6.2 feet tall. So, this shows some bias in terms of how we perceive a CEO should look like.

Kala (Time) – Desha (Place)

Just specifying a local time (Kala) does not make sense without mentioning the place or the time zone (Desha). Thus Kala (time) and Desha (place) go together just like Nama – Rupa. All the four are man-made concepts.

Certain times of the day are more suitable for reading, praying, meditation, exercise, etc. We generally find working from dawn to dusk as convenient. Eating and sleeping at the appropriate time is good for health.

Desha has its own effect on our perception and behavior depending on the place we are at. For example, our mindset and actions are different depending on whether we are at home, office, customer location, mall, resort, different city or different country. That's the reason for having places of worship like churches or temples because they automatically help one's mind to become quiet and to find peace within oneself.

Vedic philosophy says that one can transcend this Kala and Desha by being completely aware in the present moment or being in the "Now" so that one can bury the past and stop being anxious about the future. In the past things happened in the "Now" and in the future also things are going to happen only in the "Now". Hence the power of "Now" needs to be recognized and one should practice to live in the "Now". Definitely, we should learn from the past and should plan for the future. It is just that we need to be aware that the tendency of the mind and the ego is always to dwell in the past or to fantasize about the future, the overindulgence of which could lead to fear, stress and anxiety. Consciously practicing to stay in the present moment forces the mind to remain calm, renders the ego powerless and allows one to enjoy serenity, peace, quietude and beatitude.

Outer World Summary

The Outer World provides the stimuli and inputs to the mind which are received by it through the five sense organs. These inputs if not found relevant or interesting, the mind discards them. Otherwise, these inputs of the "Outer World" through assimilation, discrimination and synthesis get interpreted by the mind and they go on to contribute to the modifications of the ever-changing "Inner World".

Thus, whatever happens in the Outer World has an impact on the Inner World inside our mind. In the same way, we have an impact on the world around us with whatever feelings, emotions and beliefs we carry.

Every one of us likes to be happy. Nobody wants to say "I want to be unhappy". Since the sense organs are always directed outwards, we always tend to seek happiness from the outer world. Though the objective is to seek happiness we actually go after seeking pleasure. Every pleasure comes wrapped with several layers of cover which need to be unraveled using series of actions before we can enjoy the pleasure, albeit momentarily and not continuously.

For example, to taste a good dish, we need to engage in several actions like going to a shop to purchase all the groceries, start the cooking, follow all the procedures of that recipe and finally have the dish in a plate ready to be relished. As we start eating bite by bite, if the dish has come out well as expected then we start savoring it, enjoying the pleasure and experiencing the happiness. This no one can deny. But the important question that needs to be asked is, "Does the happiness really lie in that dish?" The initial answer may be "Yes". We did experience the happiness. If one understands the question properly and still the answer is "Yes", then it implies that the dish gave the happiness. If that were to be true, then one would continue eating for hours together because why should one be contented with limited happiness? Instead, one could continue eating and experience unlimited happiness. We know from our experience that this is not the case.

Let us consider another example, say we are interested in owning certain property because we believe that it is of strategic importance to us, we could utilize it effectively and benefit immensely. After a few years of waiting finally let us say that property becomes available for the budget we have in mind. We strike the deal and succeed in getting hold of the papers. Our long-nurtured desire is achieved and we feel immensely happy. In this case, does the happiness lie in that piece of land? If so would anybody sell their happiness for money? The person who sold also seems to be happy for the price it fetched. If the happiness was really contained in that piece of land, nobody would even think of parting with it.

From the above examples, it should be clear that the real happiness did not lie in the objects of the Outer World such as a dish or a property. But it is true that in both cases the happiness was experienced. Then where did it come from? It actually came from within. Where exactly from within? From the Atman, the Self whose nature itself is happiness and bliss.

That too we experienced just a small spray of happiness that spilled out from the ocean of happiness we all contain.

Ramana Maharshi says that when a desire surfaces such as to taste a dish or to possess a property, our mind gets into a state of agitation. As the desire gains strength, the mind becomes restless and its agitations force us to engage in a series of actions. In the case of a dish, after enduring the mental agitations for a few days we might decide to act and within a few hours the dish gets prepared and we get to satisfy our desire. In the case of property, it might take months or years to achieve the goal. When the goal is achieved, at that moment for a very brief period the mental agitations completely stop and when the mind becomes absolutely quiet it allows us to experience the Self, Atman which results in happiness. Every single time we are happy, we are actually realizing our own happiness which we always carry within ourselves but always try to attribute it to an object of our desire.

"Everything is dear to us because of the Atman, the Self", says the Brihad Aranyaka Upanishad (2.4.5). Atman, our own Self is the true focus of love. Everything in the Outer World appears loveable only if it contributes to "our" satisfaction. Our Self, Atman is ever satisfied. It is the disturbance in our mind that conceals this ever-satisfied nature of the Self, says Swami Ranganathananda. Instead of searching for momentary happiness in the Outer World, we could learn to immerse in the ocean of Bliss that is within us.

According to Vedic philosophy, everything in the Outer World is for us to experience and realize the fleeting, temporary and momentary happiness they provide. To be free from any kind of worry, pain or suffering and to experience permanent happiness, the Vedic texts ask us to turn our attention inwards towards the **Sentient Life Energy,** the Self, the Atman and exist as a mass of Consciousness or exist as **Silent Awareness.**

Mind Summary

"You have power over your mind – not outside events. Realize this, and you will find strength."

– Marcus Aurelius

Every individual possesses a unique combination of Inner World, Personality, Ego, Arishadvarga (six passions) and Pancha Kleshas (five afflictions). Because of these, for a same given circumstance in the Outer World, the mind of each individual analyzes it differently and hence each person's reaction is also different.

If we consider the Personality as an *"angle"* from which a person views, the Arishadvargas are like *"glasses"* of different colors and shades and the Pancha Kleshas are the different levels of inherent *"defects"* we carry. The combination of "angle", "color shades" and "inherent defects" are unique to each individual and they skew the comprehension. That's why each one views the same thing in the Outer World differently and is unable to see the things as they are. All the components mentioned above combine to distort the vision with which we view the Outer World. As if this is not enough, the impressions we carry in our Inner World, our Personality shaped by Prarabdha Karma, Vasanas, Environment, Education and Experience, all combine to create a bias and the Ego acts as a veil and all of this further cloud our mental cognition. All these components combine to form our beliefs, opinions, predispositions, affinities, likes and dislikes with which we interact with the Outer World. Scientific research has also recognized this and calls it as "Unconscious Bias" which significantly influences our understandings and decisions.

According to Swami Chinmayananda, the body, the mind and the intellect are the instruments given to us to interact and transact with the world. We are supposed to be the masters of these instruments. When we succumb to the bodily addictions and are unable to control the desires of the mind and the dictates of our intellect, then these instruments become our masters and refuse to budge or relinquish their powers. Our endeavor should be to diminish the dominance of these instruments and become free from their clutches by strengthening our wisdom, application of our knowledge and using our common sense.

The tendency of the mind is to generate thoughts incessantly. Thoughts by themselves do not have any power if we allow them to just come and go. Only when we associate with them and show interest, the thoughts get energized and gain power. Once the thoughts gain enough power and flex their muscles, our mind starts getting agitated and becomes restless. If the thoughts are about some desires or dislikes, we get forced to engage in actions to satisfy the desires or to get rid of the things we dislike.

Thoughts often tend to be about the past or about the future. If they are unpleasant, they cause fear and anxiety. The ego is the culprit that forces the innocent mind to engage in the continuous generation of the thoughts. The ego feeds off the power and the effect it has on one's mind. More the effect, stronger the ego becomes and results in more number of thoughts. This is where the power of "Now", being in the "Present Moment" would help immensely. Instead of thinking about numerous things we want to do in the future, we should clearly think about the one thing that we want to do "Now". Practicing to be in the present moment avoids unwanted thoughts, enables us to feel the energy we carry inside which is the life force that keeps us alive, sharpens our keenness and alertness, and be fully aware by constantly staying in touch with our Consciousness or **Silent Awareness.**

Negative thoughts cause worry and increase our stress. We are aware that some negative thoughts we might have had in the past are no longer bothering us in the present moment. In the same way, the current worries also will pass away. An age-old adage says, *"And, this too, shall pass away"* and on this statement, the Wikipedia says, *"How much it expresses! How chastening in the hour of pride! How consoling in the depths of affliction!".*

Nowadays it has become common to hear about work-related tension and stress. Can a doctor be worried if over a period of time the number of patients visiting the clinic has increased along with the increase in the varied number of diseases that need to be diagnosed? Can a restaurant owner be worried because of the large number of customers visiting on a daily basis? In the same way, irrespective of whether we are a professional, running a business, have started a venture or for that matter any work we do for our living, we need to constantly expect the various challenges to pop up and strive to come up with appropriate solutions every single time. That's the reason why we get paid and are able to earn our living. There is no point in allowing the problems related to work to disturb our mental peace, constantly take away the precious time from our family and overwhelm us with stress and worries.

A leader should take the necessary measures to ensure that the team members are not stressed. In the "Pancha Klesha Summary" section we discussed how an inefficient person if happens to lead the team could breed inefficiency. Such incompetent people for the lack of talent, encourage people working after office hours, during night times, during holidays, expect team members to be available at beck and call, etc. These things should not be a consideration at all. Only the talent and merit should be the criteria. The work produced should speak. In fact, it is essential that everyone practices and develops the skill to handle the work within the assigned working hours except for emergencies and exigencies.

It is paramount that everybody on a daily basis gets adequate rest and abundant quality time with the family so that they can come back for work the next day with freshness, renewed vigor and brimming with enthusiasm. People in prominent positions such as Directors and Senior Vice Presidents should ensure that they always choose an efficient leader for every team after carefully scrutinizing all the past works done and ascertaining the leadership and execution skills. Data should be relied upon and not on opinions and perceptions.

In our Inner World, we saw that the thoughts are always about one of the four things, Vyakti (person), Vastu (object), Vishaya (topic) and Ghatana (incident). If the thoughts are positive and pleasant, we have no complaints. It is the negative thoughts that cause worries and more often such negative thoughts are always about a Vyakti since there is an increased influence of feelings, emotions and ego. In fact, while thinking about a Vyakti all the components of the mind which we have studied so far, such as our Personality, Ego, Arishadvarga and Pancha Klesha come into play. The next worrisome thoughts are about Vastu which if critically analyzed ultimately boils down to profit or loss, possession or dispossession, have it or do not have it. The thoughts about Ghatana that could cause worries are much less when compared to Vyakti and Vastu. The intensity of the worry would be more if the thoughts about Vastu and Ghatana are linked to Vyakti. For example, if we lost some possession due to somebody, or due to someone we had to face an embarrassment, then the hurt felt is more as the influence of ego and emotions are more.

Generally, the thoughts about Vishaya (topic) do not cause worries because unlike Vyakti, the thoughts about Vishaya are abstract in nature and hence the emotions and ego take a back seat. Thinking about a pure Vishaya is what inventors and discoverers indulge in. Such thoughts are a source of joy as we have seen that they are not laced with emotions nor do they involve one's ego. Regarding Vishaya, even the failed ideas do not cause dejection or depression. Instead, the failures give more insights and make one reattempt the idea with renewed vigor. The thoughts about a Vishaya make one feel enthusiastic, the thinking happens with a clear mind and encourages one's creativity to come to the fore. Thinking about the solutions to the problems at work, coming up with ways to improve the efficiency, techniques to increase the productivity, etc. can be motivational and inspirational. The habit of getting involved in abstract things does bring pure joy like music, dance, painting, sports, reading, writing, etc., as our ego is not involved in such indulgence.

The objective is to keep the worries away, reduce the sway of the ego and prevent emotions from running amok. We should try, find out and adopt the methods that help us succeed in achieving this most important objective.

Unconscious Bias

Researchers say that we all have "Unconscious Bias" because of which we routinely and rapidly sort people into our groups, "in-group" or "out-group" without being aware that we're doing it. This bias or prejudice happens due to the combination of our personality, ego, emotions, feelings, likes, dislikes, opinions, beliefs and predispositions. Our mind does the sorting in less than a second. The preferences bypass our normal, rational and logical thinking. Research confirms that everybody has this Unconscious Bias and everybody's bias is different. The types of Unconscious Bias are Conformity Bias, Beauty Bias, Affinity Bias, Halo Effect, Horns Effect, Similarity Bias, Contrast Effect, Attribution Bias and Confirmation Bias.

The HR departments of many corporates have taken this seriously as the bias may result in hiring a wrong candidate and on the other hand, might also result in not hiring a right candidate. To cut the effect of this bias, the HR departments send the document on Unconscious Bias every time along with the candidate's resume to each interviewer.

It is better to have the knowledge about this Unconscious Bias so that we become aware that the opinions and judgements we form could be wrong and we should start challenging our thoughts that are irrational and illogical.

Jagat Mithya – World is an Illusion

As our sense organs are directed outside, we always try to seek pleasure outside and try to obtain it in the outer world. Our interactions with the outer world affect our inner world and make our minds engage in ceaseless thoughts. Regarding the outer world, the great Vedic master Sri Adi Shankaracharya, who lived in the early part of the 8th Century says, *"Brahma satya jagat mithya, jivo brahmaiva naparah"*. It means Brahman (name of the Ultimate Reality) is the only truth, the world is illusory, and there is ultimately no difference between the individual Self and the Brahman.

Mithya means neither true nor false. The world cannot be false because we all clearly see and perceive it. Shankaracharya says that the world is not true either, because it is constantly changing and everything that the world has to offer is temporary, transient and impermanent.

A fine dining experience gives us joy. Try doing it continuously for a few days and one would start nauseating. A trip to a nice resort is highly relaxing. After just a few days the charm of the place wears out. Eagerly awaited vacation trip to someplace, after hectic running around and visiting various tourist sites for days, finally the heart cries "Home! Sweet Home!!" and longs for the comfort of the home.

That's why Shankara calls this world as Mithya which means anything in this world can only give temporary happiness and not permanent happiness.

For example, if we consider the simple math 2 + 2 = 4, it holds good for all times, at all places, never changes and hence is regarded as the truth. This is not the case with all the experiences that the outer world can provide. We do not remember what we did at the same time yesterday, last month or last year. We do remember some incidents pleasant or painful if they had cast some impression on us. In both the cases, it is due to the ego, either it got flattered or it got badly hurt. If we develop the mental maturity and cast aside our ego, even such incidents also would fade away from our memory.

We forget the happenings in our dream very quickly. The experience we have in the waking world also we do forget but slowly over the time. This is what is conveyed by the adage *"And, this too, shall pass away"*. This temporariness, irrelevance, impermanence of everything related to the outer world and the similarity of the experience with the dream world is what made Shankara term the world as neither false nor real, but illusory and need not be given any importance apart from what is required practically to transact.

In saying "Jivo brahmaiva naparah", Shankara is conveying that the realization of the individual Self, Atman, Life Energy in its purest form (without the ego) is nothing but realizing the Brahman, the Almighty Energy. The same opinion is echoed by the ancient Greek aphorism "Know Thyself" which is inscribed in the Temple of Apollo at Delphi. These sayings assert that one learns more by studying oneself (Svadhyaya) by making the mind calm and quiet and directing the single-pointed concentration inwards.

Chapter 2
Vivekas

"We cannot solve our problems with the same thinking we used when we created them"

– Albert Einstein

KNOWLEDGE IS POWER

❧ ❧ ❧

Om Asato Maa Sad-Gamaya.
Tamaso Maa Jyotir-Gamaya
Mrtyor Maa Amritam-Gamaya
Om Shaanti Shaanti Shaantihi

Om, Lead me from unreal to real.
Lead me from darkness (of ignorance) to light (of knowledge).
Lead me from death to immortality.
Om, Peace, Peace, Peace.

❧ ❧ ❧

Vivekas - Reasonings

"The true function of philosophy is to educate us in the principles of reasoning and not to put an end to further reasoning by the introduction of fixed conclusions."

– George Henry Lewes

Viveka (reasoning) means discriminating after doing the **Vichara** (enquiry) which is engaging in the required thinking, contemplation and reasoning. Our discerning mind can identify, recognize and categorize the good and bad, useful and harmful, pleasure and pain, happiness and sorrow, light and darkness, etc. Swami Tejomayananda says Viveka means using the same distinguishing and reasoning faculty of the intellect to enquire into various relationships such as the means and the goal (Sadhana-Sadhya Viveka), the part and the whole (Amsa-Amsi Viveka), the eternal and the ephemeral (Nithya-Anithya Viveka), etc. **This chapter on "Vivekas" is the crux of this book.**

The Greek philosopher, Heraclitus of Ephesus proclaimed *"The only thing that is Constant is Change"*. Plato later echoed the same by saying *"Everything changes and nothing stands still"*. Upon very simple enquiry we also realize that everything around us is continuously changing. People and objects around us change, friends and relationships change, jobs, colleagues and companies change and so do the economic, political and social environments. We see ever-evolving changes in our culture, customs, fashions, lifestyles, education, technology, gadgets, entertainment, transport, etc. From the subatomic to the cosmic level, everything in this universe is perennially in a state of flux.

Our own views and opinions change, likes and dislikes change, knowledge and understanding change, the moods of the mind change and of course, our body is constantly changing. Where is the less than 2 feet body we had when we were born? Where is the little under 3 feet body we had when we were toddlers? Those bodies are gone and the body we have now is of different height and weight, which again has not stopped changing.

It makes us wonder whether everything is impermanent? Is there anything permanent? For this fantastic all important philosophical question we need not have to seek the answer from elsewhere. The wisdom required to provide the answer lies very much within you. With just a little cooperation and effort from you, we shall together stumble upon the right answer.

It is not that difficult to understand that your body has been continuously changing as you did possess different bodies at different points in time ever since you were born. In all those different bodies since your infancy, were you not the same person who inhabited those bodies including the body you have now? The **Sentient Life Energy,** the Self, the real "I" which had powered those bodies is still the same and is powering the current body we possess. The **Sentient Life Energy** that gives us life every moment has never changed and never changes. This life energy is sentient which means it has consciousness or rather it is Consciousness itself. Vedic philosophy says using the feeling of "I" we should identify ourselves with the **Sentient Life Energy** or our Consciousness or our Awareness. Instead, we wrongly identify "I" with our ego, name and form. We wrongly identify "I" with our body, mind and intellect.

Ever since we were born, the body has changed, the mind has changed and the intellect has changed. But this Sentient Life Energy, the Self, the real "I" has never changed. It is I who went to school, the same I who went to college and it is the same I who is reading this book. Voila, we have stumbled upon the answer. It is this "I", the Self which has never changed in our life even though everything else around us has been continuously changing.

Viveka means using the reasoning to ultimately grasp this "I", the Self, Swayam Prakasha (self-luminous), the dazzling Truth, the resplendent Reality, the changeless Eternity, the mountain of Peace and the ocean of Bliss. Basking in this thought of Self and delighting in its glory is the ultimate goal of the path shown by the Vedic literature.

In this chapter "Vivekas" (reasonings), four different reasonings are explained to realize the same Sentient Life Energy, Consciousness, Awareness, Atman. The different Vivekas are Drig-Drishya (seer-seen), Pancha Kosha (five sheaths), Traya Avasta (three states) and Mahavakya (great sayings). The different reasonings help us understand so that we can stop the wrong identification of "I" with our ego, name and form and start identifying ourselves with the real "I" which is the Sentient Life Energy, Consciousness, Awareness or Atman.

One may wonder what is the point of understanding this unchanging "I"? What purpose does it serve? We shall strive to seek the answers to these puzzling questions before we end this chapter.

Drig-Drishya Viveka

Drig-Drishya Viveka (Seer-Seen Viveka) is an enquiry into the distinction of the Seer (Drig) and the Seen (Drishya), the Knower and the Known, the Perceiver and the Perceived, the Witness and the Witnessed. This is considered as one of the most important pieces of work in the Vedic literature and contains just forty-six slokas (verses). Certain verses of Katha Upanishad (2.6.7) and Bhagavad-Gita (3.42) convey the essence of Drig-Drishya Viveka. In Drig-Drishya Viveka, in the very first sloka itself the entire Viveka is explained.

The witness witnesses the scene, the witness is distinctly different from the scene and the witness is never affected by the scene. This is the nature of the witness which we all are aware of.

When the eyes see various objects, the pair of eyes is the seer and the objects are the seen. We can also say the eyes are the witness and the objects are the witnessed.

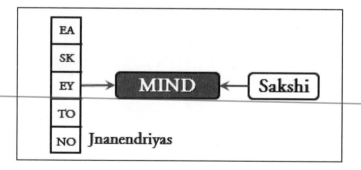

Just like the **EY**es, all other Jnanedriyas (sense organs) **EA**r, **SK**in, **TO**ngue and **NO**se are the perceivers and the respective sense objects are the perceived.

Drig-Drishya Viveka further explains that eyes and other sense organs are pretty much useless without the **MIND** being present. The mind is very much required to process the input provided by the eyes. In this case, the mind is the witness and the various inputs provided by the eyes as well as other sense organs are the witnessed.

Let us continue the exploration further. The mind continuously processes numerous inputs and incessantly generates various thoughts. Though the mind undergoes these various modifications we are also conscious of the mind's activities. This Consciousness or the Self is the **SAKSHI** (Witness) and the various activities and thoughts of the mind are the witnessed.

The Self is never witnessed or perceived by any other entity. The Self is Swayamprakasha (self-luminous) and does not undergo any change but witnesses all the changes and modifications of the mind. This witnessing Consciousness does not rise, nor does it set; It does not increase, nor does it decrease; It shines by itself without any external aid.

The Self powers the mind and we use the mind for all kinds of thoughts. In this noise of thoughts, the Self gets hidden and acts as a mute witness. When this noise is eliminated with indifference to the thoughts, the mind becomes absolutely quiet. With such a quiet mind if there is a steadfast single-pointed concentration on the Self, then the mind allows the Self to be experienced. Just like we as a third person observe something outside, in the same way, we need to observe our own mind.

For example, when I am angry, I may be completely involved in that emotion and shouting at somebody angrily. At that moment I am also aware that I am angry. That awareness is not involved or affected by the anger and acts as a mute witness.

I may be watching an interesting movie and be completely immersed in it. Yet I am conscious that I am watching a movie. That consciousness is completely dispassionate and not involved or affected by the movie and acts as a mute witness.

Similarly, I may be playing a game and be totally engrossed in it. Still, I am conscious that I am playing a game. That consciousness is not involved or affected by the happenings of the game and acts as a mute witness.

Thus, in every activity, whether I am happy, sad, angry, cheerful, suffering, etc. I may be completely involved in that emotion, yet at the same time I am also aware of the state of my mind. This Awareness is the Silent Witness, which never changes, is ever present and is not affected by any emotion.

On a screen when a movie is projected, one gets to see all kinds of scenes which are happy, sad, horrifying, etc. Though the screen is the substratum onto which the movie was projected, the screen just remains as a witness and is unaffected by the happenings in the movie. In the same way, our Awareness is the witness to all our emotions of the mind and activities of the body and remains unaffected by them. If thoughts, desires and emotions arising in the mind are cognized as objects, then they become the seen and the seer of these thoughts is the Awareness which is the ever-present Sakshi (Witness). A calm and quiet mind is required to fully experience the Silent Awareness.

Drig-Drishya Viveka Summary

According to Vedic philosophy, the mind is an inert object. It gains its sentient nature (Kena Upanishad 1.5) when it gets illuminated by the self-luminous, self-effulgent Self, the life force, the Chit Shakti (Sentient Energy), the Awareness or the Consciousness. We need to first understand the Self using the mind by doing Vichara (enquiry) and finally reach and abide in the Self using the same mind again by doing Sadhana (practice and implementation) (Katha Upanishad 2.4.11).

Science calls it as mind while the Vedic literature calls it as **Antahkarana** which literally means the Inner Instrument. This inner instrument used for thinking is said to be comprised of four components, **Manas** (mind), **Buddhi** (intellect), **Chitta** (memory) and **Ahamkara** (ego).

- **Manas** (mind) is nothing but thoughts. Manas is the seat of desires, emotions, moods, likes, dislikes, etc., and is responsible for hasty decisions and knee-jerk reactions. Manas keeps changing as we know that the thoughts we had a few years back are entirely different from the thoughts we have in the present moment.

- **Buddhi** (intellect) is the decision-making thoughts. Buddhi is a refined form of Manas and is responsible for reasoning, observation, conclusion, discrimination, logical thinking, hypothesis, ideas, creativity, etc. People who rely more on Buddhi are calm and collected, and are called rationalists. The Buddhi also keeps changing as we clearly know that the knowledge and the wisdom we possess have been changing over the years.

- **Chitta** (memory) is the store-house like a computer hard drive and is responsible for recollection, reflection and analysis. Chitta is used to store all the knowledge we learn and the experience we gain. Any event or incident that has impacted us irrespective of whether it is pleasant or painful is stored in Chitta. The Chitta is also changing as the things that were considered important and stored by the memory in the past are not the same when compared to our present interests.

- **Ahamkara** (ego) is the sense of individuality provided by the "I" thought. Ahamkara is closest to the Self and connects the Self to our body, mind and intellect. When we say "I am tall", we are referring to the body, "I am sad", we are referring to the mind and when we say "I have an idea", we are referring to the intellect. Ahamkara gives rise to the feeling "I am the doer" and provides a strong notion of doership in every act or deed of ours. Though the Ahamkara is the feeling of "I" and does not mean pride, if uncontrolled, it becomes the main cause for the pride. Unlike the other three, Manas, Buddhi and Chitta, the Ahamkara which is the feeling of "I", never changes.

Then is the changeless Ahamkara the Self? No. Though the Ahamkara gives the feeling "I", it refers to the lower self, the ego and not the Self. Sages call this Ahamkara as an illusion which deludes the individual in inflating the ego and overidentification of the "I" thought with the mind and the body.

Ramana Maharshi says that neither the insentient body says "I", nor the sentient, self-effulgent, ever-present Consciousness says "I". Between them, the Ahamkara (ego) rises as "I" and ties both of them together and it is known as Chit-Jada-Granthi (Sentient-Insentient-Knot). This knot needs to be cut using the sword of reasoning and discrimination. The non-emergence of the egoistic "I" is the pure state of being. To destroy the ego, the source of its emergence has to be sought by digging deep and turning the mind inwards. Then the Ahamkara subsides and the experience of the Self emerges as the real "I" – "I" – "I".

One of the slokas in Drig-Drishya Viveka explains that the Ego, because of its proximity to the Self, confuses us by taking the nature of the Self and behaves like a heated iron ball. An iron ball is round and cold. The fire has no particular shape and is hot by nature. When the two come in contact, they transfer each other's properties. The iron ball glows red like the fire and the fire takes on the round appearance of the iron ball. This mutual transfer of properties is called Anyonya Adhyasa (mutual superimposition).

Along with the above explanation, Swami Gurubhaktananda also gives another modern example of analyzing the inter-relationship between electricity and a light bulb. The bulb becomes luminous and the electricity manifests as the light through the bulb. The idea is, if the instrument which is the bulb and its activity which is to glow, are all considered together along with the electricity then the pure nature of electricity cannot be understood. Only if the activity and the instrument namely "glowing" and the "bulb" are separated and discarded, then the real nature of the electrical energy could be understood.

In the same way, our life principle or life force or life energy powers the instruments which are our mind and the body. The activity of the mind is the thoughts and the activity of the body is engaging in various actions. When we separate and discard the instruments and their activities, which are the body and the mind, and their activities, then we can grasp, understand and experience our own life energy. Unlike the electrical energy which is inert, our life energy is sentient which means it has Consciousness, rather it is the Consciousness itself. When we abide in this Consciousness, the mind becomes quiet, we experience the silence and the ego or the individuality vanishes.

Drig-Drishya Viveka emphasizes that we need to be disinterested in the Drishya (seen) and desire to always be constantly delighted in the Drig (seer) which is nothing but experiencing the **Sentient Life Energy** by being in **Silent Awareness.**

Pancha Kosha Viveka

Pancha Kosha Viveka (Five-Sheaths Viveka) is the science of examining the five sheaths that cover the Self. This Viveka is explained in the 2nd chapter, Anandavalli section of the Taittiriya Upanishad.

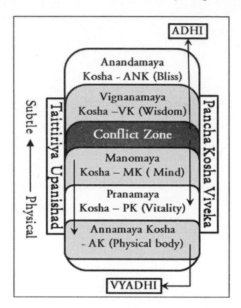

According to the Vedic philosophy the outermost sheath is **Annamaya Kosha** (Food Sheath) made up of the gross body with skin, flesh and bones → inside which resides the **Pranamaya Kosha** (Energy Sheath), the energy layer made up of vital air → inside which resides the **Manomaya Kosha** (Mental Sheath) consisting of the mind → inside which resides the **Vignanamaya Kosha** (Wisdom Sheath) representing the intellect containing the knowledge and the wisdom and gives the feeling of Kartha, the doer → inside which resides the **Anandamaya Kosha** (Bliss Sheath), the layer of bliss which gives the feeling of Bhogtha, the enjoyer.

Each sheath is subtler than its outer sheath and each sheath pervades and controls all its outer sheaths. As per Pancha Kosha Viveka, the splendor of the Self is hidden inside these five koshas, none of these five koshas are Self and if all the koshas are negated and discarded then what remains is the **Sentient Life Energy**, the Self or the Consciousness or the Awareness or the Atman.

Annamaya Kosha – Food Sheath

Annamaya Kosha (AK), the Food Sheath is made of food, represents the Sthula Sharira (gross body) consisting of skin, blood, flesh, bones, etc. "Anna" means food and "maya" means pervaded. The gross body pervaded by the modifications of food is made of Pancha Bhootas (five elements) and undergoes Shad Vikara (six transformations) namely:

1. Asti (Existence) – formation of the fetus in a mother's womb.

2. Jayate (Born) – the arrival of the baby into the world.

3. Vardhate (Growth) – the body grows being nourished by the food.

4. Viparnamate (Matures) – the body matures into adolescence, youth and attains its peak vitality.

5. Apakshiyate (Decays) – as the body ages, the decay sets in causing a reduction in its strength.

6. Vinashyati (Death) – finally the body disintegrates and merges back into the Pancha Bhootas (five elements) at the time of death.

Whenever we say "I am tall", "I am an engineer", "I am son of so and so", etc., we are referring to the Annamaya Kosha. The first sentence directly referred to the body. The second one referred to the profession done using the body (and the mind). The third sentence referred to the bodily relationship. When we use our name, it is nothing but a label given to the body for the purpose of identification and transaction.

We wrongly identify ourselves with the body which is made up of food. The wheat is not me, the flour is not me, the bread is not me, but then once it is eaten how could it become me?

The enquiry helps us to understand that we need not over-identify ourselves with the body and our name which is a label given to the body.

We need to take good care of the body which is the temple that houses the Self, Atman and we should use the body to perform useful and helpful actions.

Pranamaya Kosha - Energy Sheath

Pranamaya Kosha (PK) is the bio-energy sheath or the vital air sheath. Pranamaya Kosha along with the next two, Manomaya and Vignanamaya, all three together constitute Sukshma Sharira (subtle body).

Pranamaya Kosha consists of five modifications of the vital air which are called Pancha Pranas (five vital airs).

1. Prana – Breathing process consisting of inhalation and exhalation are governed by Prana.

2. Apana – Situated in the pelvic floor, takes care of the evacuation and removal of all waste and toxins.

3. Vyana – Situated in the lungs and heart, it is responsible for the blood circulation energizing every cell in the entire body.

4. Udana – Situated in the throat is responsible for speech, self-expression and the thoughts emerging in the mind.

5. Samana – Situated in the abdomen, governs the digestion and assimilation of food.

We actually refer to Pranamaya Kosha when we say "I am breathing fast", "I am hungry", "I am thirsty", etc.

The five pranas described above are vital to life and the vital air is the link connecting the individual body to the outer world. The breath should be deep, slow and rhythmic. Whenever we are agitated, angry or anxious, the breathing becomes shallow and fast. During such times bringing our consciousness to the breath and deliberately taking a few deep slow breaths helps alleviate anger, fear and anxiety.

Manomaya Kosha – Mind Sheath

Manomaya Kosha (MK), the mental sheath, consists of the Manas (mind) and the five Jnanendriyas (organs of perception). The mind is the seat of all thoughts, emotions, feelings, desires, aversions, moods, attitudes, opinions, beliefs, etc. As we have seen already, the mind is influenced by our personality which in turn is shaped by our environment, education and experiences.

When we say "I am happy", "I am sad", "I am angry", etc. we are referring to the Manomaya Kosha which is the seat of thoughts, desires, emotions and moods.

It is really not the mind that is responsible for the generation of thoughts. It is the self-centered ego that makes the mind restless with self-centered thoughts. Through enquiry and reasoning, we need to constantly keep the ego under check, discipline the mind, nurture purity and develop a distaste for selfish thoughts and desires. The ever turbulent Manomaya Kosha cannot be the Self.

Vignanamaya Kosha – Wisdom Sheath

Vignanamaya Kosha (VK), the intellectual sheath consists of the Buddhi (intellect) and is the seat of Jnana (knowledge). Hence it is also called knowledge or wisdom sheath. As mentioned earlier the Pranamaya, Manomaya and Vignanamaya koshas together constitute Sukshma Sharira (subtle body).

When we say "I took a good decision", "I am satisfied", etc., we are referring to the Vignanamaya Kosha consisting of intellect, the decision-making faculty.

Buddhi is a vehicle for higher thought, capable of respecting and nourishing values, spurs creativity, innovation, discovery, visualization and discrimination. A well-developed intellect can control and hold the mind in a tight leash, guide and direct it in a productive manner.

Anandamaya Kosha – Bliss Sheath

Anandamaya Kosha (ANK), the Bliss Sheath is experienced in deep dreamless sleep, is established in ignorance and is of the form of Karana Sharira (causal body).

When we say "For the last few minutes I did not know what happened around me. I was in a state of bliss", we are referring to Anandamaya Kosha the layer responsible for providing the feeling of joy and happiness.

Whenever we obtain the object of our desire, we feel happy, which is nothing but a spray of happiness that trickles down from Anandamaya Kosha. For the duration of that experience, the mind is still and calm without any agitations. When the mind is still and calm, Anandamaya Kosha reveals itself so that the happiness contained in the Bliss Sheath could be experienced. Soon that happy experience ends because the mind gets back to its agitations and restlessness resulting in continuous thoughts caused by the desires due to the selfish nature of the ego.

Conflict Zone

Conflict Zone is not one of the sheaths, but an insight which we want to highlight. As shown in the figure, the Conflict Zone is a zone between the Manomaya Kosha and the Vignanamaya Kosha. When the activities of the mind are in constant conflict with the intellect, then this Conflict Zone thickens and gains in strength. When the mind proposes and though the intellect warns but nudged by the ego if the mind forcibly indulges in an action, then the associated repercussions and risks can cause doubts, fear, anxiety and stress. They breed negative thoughts like, "Should I have involved in this?", "Will my attempt succeed?", "What if it fails?", "What if someone finds out?".

Basically, the mind has forced an action or a deed which the intellect had forewarned not to indulge in. According to the yogic texts whenever the intellect, mind and the body are not aligned and fail to be in sync, this dysfunctional relationship causes mental imbalances and intense worries.

If they are not controlled, they amplify into mental illnesses called Adhi (primary disease). If still unattended they percolate down to Pranamaya Kosha creating the imbalance in the rhythm of breathing causing not sufficient prana (air) to flow in the body. If it is still not observed and treated, then these imbalances descend down to Annamaya Kosha (gross body) and appear as Vyadhi (disease).

In the modern society several diseases such as diabetes, hypertension, etc., have been traced to the stressful life disorders. Adhis (primary diseases) caused due to the disharmonious relationship of the body, mind and intellect need to be identified when they are still at the mental level and eliminated so that they do not get developed into Vyadhis (diseases). Yogic texts identify the interrelationships between the koshas to analyze the Adhis and Vyadhis and help in healing and healthy living.

In the figure, there is one more arrow from Manomaya Kosha to Annamaya Kosha. It indicates that due to the ego, the tendency of the mind is to always identify with the body and its sense organs to seek happiness. Hence the mind indulges in imaginations, daydreams and fantasies, and forces the body to engage in actions to satisfy the insatiable, irrational desires. This uncontrolled corrupting influence of the ego on the mind can cause agitations and restlessness which could result in Adhis (primary diseases) and if those mental conflicts are not eliminated, then it would result in Vyadhis (diseases) as seen above.

From the figure, it is clear that to seek happiness the mind should not come down to Annamaya Kosha. Instead, it should be turning in the opposite direction where Anandamaya Kosha (Bliss Sheath) is located. For that, the mind has to first breach the Conflict Zone to reach the Vignanamaya Kosha before it can reach the Anandamaya Kosha. Thus, if the mind is turned inwards, well aligned and synchronized with the intellect, the Conflict Zone gets torn apart, one develops contempt and distaste towards sense organs, ego gets annihilated and could start making progress towards experiencing Anandamaya Kosha.

Pancha Kosha Viveka Summary

Swami Sarvapriyananda in one of his YouTube video lectures gives a simple example to understand the five Koshas clearly. My hand with its skin, flesh, muscles, bones and blood belongs to Annamaya Kosha. When I raise my hand, the energy used to move the hand is the Pranamaya Kosha. The thought of wanting to raise the hand belongs to the Manomaya Kosha. The knowledge of how far the hand is raised, whose hand it is, which hand it is, etc., are the functions of the intellect belonging to the Vignanamaya Kosha. If there is a joy in raising the hand, say by a person after undergoing several months of physiotherapy, then that joy is coming from the Anandamaya Kosha. Though each of these five koshas wrongly try to appear as Self, when all the five koshas stand negated then what remains is the **Sentient Life Energy**, the Self, the Consciousness, the Awareness. The **Sentient Life Energy** powers all the koshas and witnesses all their activities.

After the five sheaths are understood, appreciated and set aside, still the doubt remains as to where is the Self, the Consciousness, the Awareness, the Atman. The master Vidyaranya in his masterpiece work "Pancha Dashi" (A Book of 15 Chapters) goes about addressing the doubt in a powerful manner by converting the doubt itself into the answer.

If the doubt is about where is the Self after understanding about the five sheaths, then Vidyaranya questions back by saying who understood it? If it is agreed that the five sheaths can be experienced, then who is the experiencer? He says that knower, that experiencer is verily the Self.

Next argument is that in the field of knowledge there are known objects and there are unknown objects. Let us say I know cycling well and hence it is known. I do not know skating and hence it is unknown. But there is only one knower who is always the subject and who cannot be objectified, hence cannot be an object of experience, but the experiencer itself. For example, the presence of an object or any number of objects can be ascertained by the eyes by seeing those objects. But the presence of the eyes themselves is ascertained by experiencing the ability to see. It would be ludicrous to ask for a mirror to look at so that we could look at our own eyes as another external object to confirm the presence of our eyes.

Continuing his masterclass, Vidyaranya says that if sugar is added to a glass of milk, it becomes sweet. If sugar is added to a jar of water, then it lends its sweetness to the water. To make the sugar taste sweet, we do not need to add more sugar to it as the sweetness is the inherent nature of the sugar.

Sugar + Milk = Milk becomes sweet
Sugar + Water = Water becomes sweet
Sugar + Sugar = STUPIDITY **@@%%!!!

In the same way, to become aware of the glass of milk we just need to become aware of it. Becoming aware of the milk means we know how much milk the cup contains, the shape of the container, whether the hot milk is steaming, etc. Basically, knowing everything about the milk that can be known. In the same way, if we divert our awareness or consciousness towards a TV, we become aware of the TV so that we get to know its size, color, brand, whether it is switched on or not, etc.

Consciousness + Milk = Milk becomes known
Consciousness + TV = TV becomes known
Consciousness + Consciousness = ABSURD, System Crash, Division by Zero **@@%%!!!

To know our consciousness, we cannot use or bring another consciousness. In the previous paragraph, we saw that the knower, the subject, cannot become a knowable object. So, to become aware of our awareness or to become conscious of our consciousness we do not have to do anything rather than "just be". Keeping the mind calm and just exist as a thinker without doing any thinking.

The mind is the instrument required to experience the Awareness. That's why in the deep sleep when the mind is taking rest we do not experience our Awareness. We just need to turn the mind inwards with a single-pointed concentration to become aware of our own Silent Awareness.

We discussed the same under the topic "Inner World" where we saw that the Consciousness plus Object becomes Thought. Vidyaranya says just reject the object and remain with the Consciousness which is the Self.

In the next point, Vidyaranya chides us by saying how shameful it is for a person to utter loudly that "I do not have a tongue". A person without a tongue should not be able to speak. With the tongue firmly in his cheek, Vidyaranya says that it should be considered shameful if a person with a tongue still goes ahead and makes such a statement. He says that the statement "I am not able to become aware of my Awareness" also belongs to the same shameful category.

Swami Anubhavananda says that through the mind one can only know the object of knowledge and not the knower of the object. This is like eyes can see all the external objects but can never see themselves. Thus, the impossibility of the subject ever becoming the object is established. Every single thing we know be it mathematics, science, philosophy, news, politics, sports, etc., are outside of us. We are the subject and the known is the object. We have been conditioned that way where everything we know is the object to be known, always outside of us and we are the knower.

Now the challenge is we need to know the knower which is inside us, which cannot be objectivized and that is the barrier we need to cross. The knower can only be experienced and cannot be known the way we know the objects. The knower cannot be known by the mind. We experience our seeing ability. In the same way, we just need to experience our knowing ability. Keeping the mind calm and silent, the **Sentient Life Energy** with the knowing ability, the **Silent Awareness** could be experienced.

This points to the self-illumined nature of the Awareness. Nothing else is required to experience our Awareness or to become aware of our Awareness or to abide in our **Silent Awareness.** Awareness or

Consciousness or Self or Atman, all refer to the same with different names and it is of the nature of self-existence, self-experience and self-illumination. To experience the Awareness, just be silent, become aware of your own silence and enjoy being in that **Silent Awareness.**

Traya Avasta Viveka

According to Mandukya Upanishad, a human being always exists in one of the three states which are called **Jagrat Avasta** (waking state), **Swapna Avasta** (dream state) and **Sushupti Avasta** (deep sleep state meaning dreamless sleep). Ever since we were born every single day, we are in one of these Traya Avastas (three states).

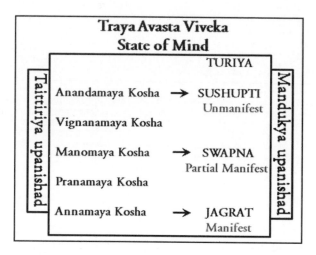

Jagrat Avasta – Waking State

In **Jagrat**, the waking state, our mind is fully active filled with thoughts, feelings and emotions, the five sense organs are in full alertness and our consciousness is focused outwards. Our ego, I and the sense of me and mine is fully manifest, is in full force and we identify ourselves with our Sthula Sharira (gross body). All our traits, characteristics, habits, personality, etc., are fully manifested. In this waking state the Consciousness is called **Vishwa** (world) and as the sense organs are always directed outwards, we try to seek pleasure from everything present in the outer world.

Swapna Avasta – Dream State

In Swapna, the dream state, only the mind is fully active and it is the mind which creates, sustains and ends the dream. The mind projects the dream world using the impressions formed from the experience of the outer world during waking state. Swami Tejomayananda says that the dreams are the unfulfilled wishes or the garbled impressions of the waking state. In the dream state, the Self or the Consciousness does not identify with the gross body, but only identifies with the Sukshma Sharira (subtle body) which consists of the mind and the intellect.

The Consciousness in the dream state is called **Taijasa** (light). Interestingly as per the name, the dreams are always well lit like a movie. In our waking state our ego is fully manifested, but in our dream state our ego is partially manifested, there is no notion of doership and hence there is no merit or demerit created in the dream. Dreams may be highly illogical with flying horses, talking animals, etc., might seem unreal to the waker, but they appear very real to the dreamer.

In the dream, everything we feel appears very real at that time. The thirst, hunger, joy, fear, etc., we experience in the dream are exactly the same way, we experience them in the waking state. In this experience, the dream state is carrying a very important message for us. If we have a frightening experience in the dream, it appears so real that we might sweat, breathe faster and sometimes we even wake up only to realize that it was just a dream and feel relieved. That means in the notion of "I" there is not much difference between the dream and waking states.

We clearly know that during the dream our gross body is completely taking rest, lying still on the bed and not playing any part in the dream. That means, for the feeling of I, the physical body is not required at all. This is the most important message that the dream state is giving us. Yet in the waking state we completely identify ourselves with the body, we even point to our body and say this is I. But the dream state is showing us that the feeling of I is unchanged in the dream and remains the same as it is in the waking state. Hence for the feeling of I, the physical body is not essential. That means the real I, *"the Self is definitely not the body, it is subtler than that"*.

Sushupti Avasta – Deep Sleep State

Sushupti is the deep sleep state, a dreamless, undisturbed, peaceful sleep, the Consciousness identifies only with the Karana Sharira (causal body). The Consciousness in this state is called **Prajna** (Consciousness, Awareness). Our ego is completely absent and all our habits, traits, characteristics, etc., are unmanifest and lie in seed form in the Karana Sharira (causal body). When we wake up, our entire character immediately manifests. That's why everyone after sleep does not wake up as a different person but as the same person who went to sleep.

In the sleep, we exist in our true nature which is pure Awareness but aware of nothing. Along with our body, our thinking faculty also takes rest and hence there is nothing to identify this Awareness. It is like a light illuminating an empty room. There are no objects to illuminate, there is nobody to notice this illumination and hence in that case we are forced to say that the light is illuminating but is illuminating the emptiness in the room.

Swami Sarvapriyananda very nicely says that in the deep sleep state there is "experience of absence" and not absence of experience. That's why when we wake up we say "I felt nothing" meaning I experienced nothing or I experienced the absence. This experience of absence happens because of the absence of ego. When the ego, I, me and mine is not there, then the mind is not disturbed as there are no thoughts, becomes peaceful and that allows the Self or the real nature of the human being to be experienced (Bhagavad-Gita 2.71).

Dream state proved to us that we feel our complete I-ness in the dream though the physical body is taking rest. Thus, it proved that "I" is not the body. In our deep sleep (Sushupti) we do not need proof from someone else that we existed. When we wake up, immediately we say "I" had a nice sleep. Thus the "I", the real Self was very much present in the deep sleep, but the entire thinking faculty was not present as it was taking rest due to the absence of the ego. This proves that "I" is not the thinking faculty and "I" is also not our ego. The dream state and deep sleep state together are

2. Vivekas – Traya Avasta Viveka | 91

proving that *"the real "I" is not the body, is not the mind, is not the intellect, is not the ego, but the Atman, Self, the Life Energy powering the body and the mind".*

Man wonders, *"I can think, therefore I exist"*. Veda thunders, *"I exist even if I cannot think"*, pointing to the deep sleep state where a person cannot think because the mind is at rest. We do exist during deep sleep though we cannot think during that time. Veda does not stop there. It goes even further and emphatically says it is not *"I can think, therefore I exist"* as proclaimed by Descartes. In fact, Veda says it is the other way around, *"I exist, therefore I can think"* pointing to the Chit Shakti (Sentient Energy), the Atman or the Self which if not present, the body and the mind are declared dead. Then where is the question of thinking? To think, the Self which is the real "I" should exist. One of the critiques of Descartes, the Danish philosopher Soren Kierkegaard says that the first part of the statement, "I think" itself presupposes the existence of "I" rendering the second part "therefore I exist" redundant. Vedanta says that the presupposed "I" is nothing but the Self, Atman, Consciousness or the Life Energy.

It appears as though the views of Descartes and Vedic philosophy are diametrically opposite. Actually, they are much closer than one could imagine. From where Descartes had reached it is not even a leap but a very very tiny step to reach the point of Vedanta. Descartes to his credit had touched the peak a human mind could reach by saying, "I think, therefore I am". Antoine Leonard Thomas gave it a fuller form by saying, "Since I doubt, I think; since I think, I exist". All Vedanta is asking is "who is the doubter?", "who is the thinker?". Know the doubter. Know the thinker. In the previous section "Pancha Kosha Summary", the great master Vidyaranya urges us to "Know the Knower".

Vedanta is asking us to realize that a doubter can exist without any doubt. A thinker can exist without any thought. A knower can exist without knowing anything in particular. A thinker to think the mind is required. A thinker to exist without thinking, the mind is not required, rather a calm mind is required. This may be called as leaving the mind behind, ignoring the mind or transcending the mind. A thinker can comprehend the mind, but the mind cannot comprehend the thinker (Kena Upanishad 1.1–1.3, Brihad Aranyaka Upanishad 3.7.20, 3.8.11). We need to leave the domain of "thinking" and enter the domain of "experiencing", "existing" and "being". Just exist as a thinker without doing any thinking, devoid of any thought. Exist as **Sentient Life Energy** being in Silent Awareness.

The deep sleep state is natural to every one of us and we experience it on a daily basis. In this natural phenomenon which we all experience every night, Nature is silently screaming and trying to tell us some important messages and Nature's silent scream is actually deafening. From time immemorial, for every single human being, there are some very profound truths Nature is relentlessly trying to tell through our deep sleep experience, but we have not been paying attention to them. At least now let us try to wake up and find out what those truths are.

After a nice long deep sleep when we wake up, do we feel terrible or do we say the sleep was blissful? We never ask this question. After we wake up, we say, "I had a very nice sleep" and forget about it. For example, a dessert which may be a pudding or ice-cream, we might enjoy it and feel good. After that, we just forget about it. But if we question ourselves why the dessert felt good, then it gives us knowledge. Why did it feel good? It felt good because it was sweet. Where did the sweetness come from? From the sugar which was added to the dessert. Simple, the entire truth now stands revealed.

In the same way, after we wake up if we question why the sleep felt good, then the message which Nature is trying to give us would get revealed. Why did the sleep feel good? The sleep felt good because it was extremely peaceful. How did we get the peace? It was peaceful because there were absolutely no thoughts. During deep sleep, I did not know who owes me or whom I owe. I did not know about my bank balance or the loan and EMI I have to repay. I did not know about my profession. I did not know about the place or the city where I was sleeping. I did not know about my religion or nationality. I did not know about my parents, siblings or children. For that matter in the deep sleep, I did not know whether

I am a male or female. Though all the reasons given above are true, they are only symptoms and not the real reasons. The real reason is *"I did not have my ego"* in the deep sleep. When the ego is dropped, all the symptoms discussed so far materialize and finally results in the experience of peaceful bliss.

When we wake up, we always say, "I slept happily". Happiness resulted because in the deep sleep the ego gets automatically dropped. In a mathematical equation, we say LHS (left-hand-side) is equal to RHS (right-hand-side) and if we have one, we can get the other. Trying to express our findings as an equation we can say dropping the ego is the LHS and its result which is happiness is the RHS.

Drop the Ego = Happiness

If all the time we want the RHS, which is to remain in happiness continuously, all we need to do is drop the ego. This is what the deafening silence of Nature is trying to tell every human being every single time when we fall into deep sleep.

For now, let the theory be clear which is *"**to remain in happiness shed the ego**"*. How to shed this ego deliberately while in waking state, we shall see as we go further. Amazingly it is not such a difficult task, thanks to the Vedanta and the amazing amount of work done by great Vedic scholars.

Every night when we go into deep sleep, the ego automatically vanishes and when we wake up, the ego automatically comes back. We can rephrase it as every night when we go into deep sleep our ego is automatically crucified and when we wake up, it gets automatically resurrected. But only if during our waking state once for all we manage to deliberately crucify our ego then the real "I", the Self would get resurrected. To remind us about this great Truth can there be any better symbolism than the crucifixion and resurrection of Jesus Christ?

Sinners are not relieved from the continuous pain and suffering with an occasional piece of temporary pleasure and happiness thrown around. Hey, but that's what is the experience of every human life and the Vedanta says that the pain and suffering are due to the ego. According to Vedanta, we are not sinners but children of one single divinity which is the **Sentient Life Energy**. The sin being committed is not realizing our own divinity and not existing in our purest (godly) form which is selflessness, love and compassion. It is this simple. This is the knowledge and discrimination. Vedanta says that the key to get delivered from our sins lies within ourselves, which is, using the sword of knowledge and discrimination, annihilate the ego so that the 'Self' shines in its fullest glory, crucify the ego so that the dazzling 'Self' could be resurrected. If we clearly understand this method of getting delivered from our sins then the statement "Jesus died for our sins" springs to life with profound meaning.

My waking world is different from yours. My dream world is different from yours. But my deep sleep state (Sushupti) and your deep sleep state are the same. Sushupti is one and the same for all. In deep sleep, a king loses the kingship; A beggar loses the poverty; A blind person loses the blindness; A person with eyes loses the sight; A terrorist loses his terrorism; A noble person loses his nobility; A lion loses its ferociousness; A rabbit loses its timidity; A deer loses its fear. Thus, Sushupti is the same for all. Why so? Because we all lose our ego and hence lose our individuality. So, Nature is silently trying to tell us how every one of us could feel one and the same but due to the presence of our ego, we do not feel the oneness.

In deep sleep, Nature is showing us the Oneness and the Unity in Diversity. In deep sleep: a Christian loses his Christianity; a Muslim forgets that he is a Muslim; a Hindu or Sikh or Buddhist or for that matter everybody loses the religion in the deep sleep. The reason is, everybody is forced by Nature to drop the ego in the deep sleep which results in the feeling of oneness. Dropping the ego means losing our individuality and start seeing oneness in everybody. A child in its infancy smiles at everybody. It does not know its or others' religion, caste, creed or nationality. The child simply smiles at everybody because it does not have the ego or its ego is not fully developed. As the child grows, from the Universal Person

(Vishwa Manava) it becomes a Limited Person (Alpa Manava) because the ego becomes fully developed resulting in the loss of oneness.

Refining the LHS and RHS of our earlier equation, we can say the LHS still remains the same which is the dropping of the ego. But RHS became enriched further which is along with the Happiness we also get Peace, Oneness and Unity in Diversity. Brihad Aranyaka Upanishad (4.3.21–4.3.32) conveys the same.

Drop the Ego = Happiness + Peace + Oneness + Unity in Diversity

So just drop the ego, be in the **Silent Awareness** and experience the Blissful Peace, Oneness and Unity in Diversity. This state of dropping the ego and experiencing the silent Consciousness is called **Turiya**, the fourth state (Mandukya Upanishad 1.7) which is actually the underlying substratum of all the three states; waking, dreaming and deep sleep states.

Mahavakya Viveka

Mahavakyas are the "Great Sayings" contained in the Upanishads where each saying contains the entire essence of the Upanishads expressed tersely and concisely. Shuka Rahasya Upanishad exclusively deliberates on these "Great Sentences" and conveys that they should be deeply understood and contemplated upon. The four principal Mahavakyas are from four Upanishads taken from each of the four Vedas. All the sayings convey one Universal message which is about the Brahman, Atman, Awareness, Consciousness or the Chit Shakti (Sentient Energy) we all contain and which sustains the life in every one of us.

Every moment, without any of our effort and knowledge there are several things happening within us. To mention a few, the heart beats nonstop, the respiratory system functions with its ceaseless inhalation and exhalation, digestive system functions tirelessly, etc. *Can anything in this world move or function without the help of energy?* There has to be definitely some energy within us that is responsible for all these functions. *There is indeed verily such an energy within every one of us which is also sentient and it is called Chit Shakti (Sentient Energy), Atman, Self, Consciousness, Awareness* (Aitareya Upanishad 3.1.1 – 3.1.2).

In Physics, energy must be transferred to an object for it to perform work. So, if the heart is beating and the lungs are expanding and contracting, it cannot happen without the help of energy. Now comes the most important point we are trying to make. One has to say the heart and lungs are functioning on their own without the help of any energy contradicting the Science. Otherwise, one has to acknowledge that the heart and lungs are indeed functioning with the help of energy upholding both the Science as well as Vedanta. We request the readers to take a pause, contemplate and decide one way or the other. *"Science without religion is lame, religion without science is blind"*, said Albert Einstein. This is our tenacious effort to finally make the science meet the philosophy. This is our sincere endeavor to finally make the east meet the west. The twain shall certainly meet and lovingly embrace in the realm of a philosophical sphere and joyfully resonate and reverberate with a harmonious symphony.

Science has identified electrical energy, magnetic energy, heat energy, kinetic energy, potential energy, etc., but ironically the science and the scientists have not shown adequate interest for this all-important Sentient Energy which powers our body organs every single moment. Luckily and contrastingly the study of Atman was the only energy Vedanta and Vedantins are interested in and hence we are in possession of an invaluable knowledge which they have provided for our benefit. Science is interested in *"innumerous inert and insentient"* things that are in this universe which is *"outside"* of us. Vedanta is interested in *"one and only sentient"* thing which is *"inside"* every one of us.

We can't see the electrical energy directly, but we can see it manifesting when it powers instruments like camera, microphone, speaker, crane, train, etc. In the same way, we can't see our Chit Shakti (Sentient Energy) but we can see it manifesting when it powers instruments like eyes, ears, tongue, hands, legs, heart, lungs, brain, mind, etc. (Kena Upanishad 1.1–1.8, Brihad Aranyaka Upanishad 3.4.2, 3.7.16–3.7.23, 3.8.11).

Let us say the main switch is turned off and all the instruments such as bulb, heater, refrigerator, etc., are turned on. Then when the main switch is switched on, the electrical energy instantly powers all the instruments, the bulb, heater, refrigerator, etc. and they start working at the same instant. In the same way, when we wake up from the deep sleep, the sentient energy within us instantly powers all the instruments such as hands, legs, eyes, ears, mind, etc. and they all start operating at the same instant. Kaushitaki Brahmana Upanishad (4.19) says, *"When one wakes up, just like from a blazing fire the sparks go forth in all directions, in the same way, the Life Energy rushes to all stations or positions in the body up to the end of the nails and hairs of the skin"*.

To realize the presence of any energy we need the right instrument. For example, to realize the presence of electricity, we need right instruments such as bulb or fan, a piece of wood would not work. In the same way, to realize the **Sentient Life Energy** which is Consciousness the right instrument is the calm mind (Kena Upanishad 3.1.8). If we have the ego, the selfish and self-centered thoughts do not allow the mind to be calm, it becomes restless and the **Sentient Life Energy** remains hidden from us. Using a quiet mind, simply existing as a mass of Consciousness or as **Silent Awareness** is the path shown by the Vedic philosophy to experience our own **Sentient Life Energy.**

We cannot "see", "think" or "comprehend" any energy. But we can directly experience or indirectly see the energy manifest when right instruments become available. Nobody can say, "show" me the gravitational energy. Nobody can "think" and "comprehend" gravitational energy. But everybody can experience the gravitational energy. Just jump in the air. You are landing back on the ground due to the gravitational energy. In the same way, life energy cannot be "shown" (Mundaka Upanishad 3.1.8, Svetasvatara Upanishad 4.20). Nobody can "think" and "comprehend" this life energy (Kena Upanishad 1.5).

Bhagavad-Gita (2.21–2.25) describes this life energy as indestructible, eternal, unborn, undecaying, can't be cut by a weapon, can't be burnt by fire, can't be wetted by water, can't be dried by air, beyond modification and beyond thought. If we do not use the word "Energy" then it necessitates this kind of adept verbal dance and nifty wordplay to make one understand and Vedic literature is proficient at it.

Every energy is experienced differently. By jumping in the air and landing back on the ground, we experience the gravitational energy. To experience the heat energy, just feel it using the skin. To experience the light energy, just see it using the eye as the instrument. In the same way, to experience the life energy, we need to make use of its sentience and the instrument required is the calm mind. Unlike other energies which are inert, the life energy is sentient. It means the life energy has the ability to know, it is Awareness, it is Consciousness, it is Sentience (Aitareya Upanishad 3.1.2, Kaivalya Upanishad 1.21). The Vedic literature says one of the natures of the life energy is Chit, meaning Consciousness or Sentience (Svetasvatara Upanishad 3.11, 3.13). So, to experience the **Sentient Life Energy,** just exist as a mass of Consciousness or as **Silent Awareness.** Lose the identification with the body, name or ego. "Just be" in the **Silent Awareness.** Dropping the ego, without any thought, being in silence, experiencing the Silent Awareness is the way to experience our **Sentient Life Energy.** If you have understood clearly what has been explained so far then jump in the air again. This time to express the delight, ecstasy and joy of successfully finding, clearly understanding and blissfully experiencing our own captivating Self, Atman, Awareness, Consciousness, the **Sentient Life Energy.**

Alas, science has made extensive research on every single organ in the body including the brain and has studied the mind too but has stopped short of exploring this life energy that is powering all the organs in the body. Unlike electrical energy which is *"inert"*, our life energy is *"sentient"* which means it has Awareness or rather the Awareness itself.

The first law of Thermodynamics states that energy can neither be created nor destroyed. That's exactly what the Vedanta also says which is the Atman, the Sentient Life Energy which we all possess is Nityam (Eternal) (Katha Upanishad – 1.2.18, Bhagavad-Gita 2.20–2.21) meaning it can neither be created nor destroyed. Electrical energy is eternal, but a bulb or any instrument is not eternal. In the same way, according to Vedanta our Life Energy is eternal, but our body is not eternal. Within our own lifetime, this Life Energy has been proving its eternity to us. The bodies we had as an infant, toddler, child, teenager, etc., are gone and the body we have now is completely different from those bodies we had earlier. But this Life Energy has been the same that powered all those bodies and is powering the current body too. It has been with us every single moment without undergoing any change. How come for so long we have been blind to this fact?

Vedanta Kesari (Lion of Vedanta) roars and urges us to identify ourselves with this eternal **Sentient Life Energy,** the real "I", instead of identifying ourselves with our mortal bodies. This is what was echoed by the mantra at the beginning of this chapter which said: *"May the light of the knowledge of the Truth dawn upon us and lead us from mortality to the nectar of immortality".*

Once different water bodies were quarrelling with each other. The bottled water claimed it is great as it is potable, looking at the dirty gutter water. The lake water claimed it is great as it sustains a large number of livestock and vegetation. The moving river water contended that it is greater than the stagnant lake. The water in the ocean beamed that it is the greatest as nobody is bigger than itself. The water in a tiny puddle smilingly said: *"You all are fools fooled by your names and forms. We all are one indeed as in reality, we all are just H2O. I am you. You are me. I am within you. You are within me. We all are one"* (Isavasya Upanishad – 1.6). Finally, the knowledge dawned and everyone agreed that we all are one and the same water molecule called H2O. In the same way, we all are one and the same Sentient Energy.

Electrical energy powers instruments like bulb, radio, TV, etc. But those instruments being inert cannot realize that they are powered by the same electrical energy. In the same way, the **Sentient Life Energy** powers instruments like body, mind and intellect. But we the human beings are not inert and hence should be able to realize that it is one single Universal Life Energy that is providing life not only to the entire mankind but also to the whole animal and plant kingdoms (Kena Upanishad 4.6). Just like there cannot be two different electrical energies, in the same way, there can be only one and there cannot be two different life energies (Chandogya Upanishad 6.2.1). If this understanding is clear and if we drop the ego and identify ourselves with our **Sentient Life Energy** then we would see oneness everywhere and each one of us would be comprehensively winning this game of life hands down and would be glad to help others win it too. Can there be any greater success than this?

The energy which is making my heart beat, lungs function and keeping me alive is exactly the same within you as well as everyone. Though powered by the same electrical energy bulb, fan, and TV perform different functions and different bulbs provide a different level of brightness according to their wattage. In the same way, though powered by the same Sentient Life Energy we differ in the functions we perform and differ in the capabilities we possess. Thus, we all are not born equal and Communism misses this. We are completely free to do what we like and what comes naturally to us. But we should not forget that at the core we all are actually this silent Sentient Energy, Silent Awareness, mass of Consciousness and not our name and form. Thus, at the core we all are same and the Capitalism misses this. Ego, name and form are required to just transact and communicate. If we drop our identity with our ego, name and form, then we could see oneness in everybody.

Let us say when I was in some terrible distress of great magnitude, a person known to me helped me. Naturally, I would be very thankful and grateful to that person. I would love such a person who helped me and would love to spend any amount of time with that person whenever we meet. We just discussed how the Atman, the Self is powering each of our body organs, making them function properly, empowering us with our very *"life"* every single moment. How much grateful we should be for that Sentient Life Energy which is keeping us alive every single moment? Which one is greater, somebody providing us some great help or something providing us our very life every single moment? It is not that we should not be grateful to a person who helped us when we were in great need.

The question is if we are that grateful to such a good person who helped us, then how much we should be thankful and grateful to our own Atman which is giving us life every single moment. Contemplating on this point, irrespective of whether one is a theist or an atheist it is imperative on every one of us to be in a thankful mood to our own Atman for at least 10 minutes every single day if not more. We should not be so ungrateful and take it for granted the great Sentient Life Energy, the Chit Shakti that is keeping us alive every moment. It does not hurt, instead, it is more rewarding to just be in a silent thankful mood for a few minutes for our own Atman.

It is with these kinds of thoughts and clear understanding we should read the Mahavakyas and contemplate on each one of them.

"Prajnaanam Brahma" means "Consciousness is Brahman" mentioned in Aitareya Upanishad (3.1.3) of Rig Veda.

"Aham Brahmaasmi" means "I am Brahman" mentioned in Brihad Aranyaka Upanishad (1.4.10) of Yajur Veda.

"Tat Tvam Asi" means "Thou art That" mentioned in Chandogya Upanishad (6.8.7) of Sama Veda.

"Ayam Atma Brahma" means "This Atman (Self) is Brahman" mentioned in Mandukya Upanishad (1.2) of Atharva Veda.

All the statements are saying that we are not our name and form. We are actually the Sentient Energy which is nothing but our own Awareness, Consciousness, Self, Atman, Brahman. This Sentient Energy powers our entire body, mind and intellect. It is because of this energy we are alive. Just like the way electrical energy powers various instruments, this energy within us powers all our bodily functions such as hearing, seeing, moving, lifting, etc. But unlike electrical energy which is inert, this life energy is sentient and hence is called Prajna which means Consciousness or Awareness. Instead of identifying with our ego, name and form, the Vedanta is asking us to identify ourselves with the **Sentient Life Energy** within us, realize it as the real "I" and exist as the silent **Sentient Life Energy** or as a mass of Consciousness or as **Silent Awareness**.

I am not name and form. I am Consciousness. This is what Prajnanam Brahma means.

I am not name and form. I am the Sentient Energy. This is what Aham Brahmasmi means.

You are not name and form. You are That (Sentient Energy). This is what Tat Tvam Asi means.

I am not name and form. I am the Sentient Energy called Atman. This is what Ayam Atma Brahma means.

The purpose of Mahavakyas is to understand their deepest meaning and in our busy lives take a few moments to be in the thankful contemplative state thinking about the great Sentient Energy that is inside every one of us and keeping us alive.

Hope that the science and the scientists recognize this **Sentient Life Energy** soon and recommend its study right from the primary school level. There is no point in studying Respiratory System, Digestive System, Excretory System, etc., without acknowledging the presence of the life energy that is powering all these systems in the body and is making them function properly. Otherwise, children would think that all these systems and the body organs are functioning on their own without the help of any energy. The science will have to contradict itself by saying that in this world nothing can move or function on its own without the help of energy. However, inside the body, organs are moving and functioning on their own without the help of any energy. How silly it would be!! It is high time that the science recognizes the presence of this all-important **Sentient Life Energy.** By inclusion of a serious study of this **Sentient Life Energy** in all the books on Energy, Biology, Anatomy, Health Sciences, etc., all the books would start shining with much more meaningful exuberance.

Vivekas Summary

The different Vivekas (reasonings) of the Vedic philosophy provide different reasoning to identify the same Self, Atman, Chit Shakti (Sentient Energy), Awareness or Consciousness. Drig-Drishya Viveka calls it as Sakshi (Witness). Pancha Kosha Viveka shows how the Self is hidden inside the five sheaths and is actually the "Knower" of the five sheaths. To ascertain the presence of the eyes, we just need to see but not see anything in particular. In the same way, to grasp our **Silent Awareness** we just need to be aware but not be aware of anything in particular. Traya Avasta Viveka shows that it is the same Self slipping effortlessly between the three states. Mahavakya Viveka nudges us to contemplate on the **Sentient Life Energy** we all possess, stop the wrong identification of "I" with the ego, body and mind and practice to abide in the **Silent Awareness** without any thoughts.

Dropping the Ego

Nature by providing Peace, Oneness and Happiness in our deep sleep state is trying to tell us how to feel the same during the waking state. The answer is to drop the ego. Now the big question arises that in the waking state how to deliberately drop the ego?

Here comes the most important section of this book as it tries to explain how to go about dropping the ego in our waking state.

Actually, all of us have dropped our ego several times but we are just not aware of it. For example, when we really enjoy a movie at that moment we are not conscious of our body. We are not conscious of our bank balance. We are not aware of our religion or nationality. We are not aware of our parents or children. Thus, while enjoying the movie we drop our ego, lose our bodily conscience and just exist as a mass of awareness becoming aware of the happenings in the movie. When the movie is that much absorbing it makes us forget our ego which makes us happily say "I enjoyed the movie". So, dropping the ego results in happiness. After the movie is over, the ego comes back bringing with it all the worldly worries, wants, greed, likes and dislikes.

The same thing happens when we are absorbed in watching a game. For those few hours, we drop our ego and enjoy the game. Once the game is over the ego comes back.

In another instance, a man indulges in rock climbing or similar thrilling activity. During rock climbing, one can't afford to lose the concentration because one wrong move and it could be a matter of life and death. The risk of the bodily injury forces the person involved in the risky activity to be in complete awareness with unwavering concentration. By now it should be clear that being in full concentration, being in full awareness means losing the ego and whenever the ego is dropped, happiness results.

Watching a movie or a game, one can afford to be not in full concentration. That's why playing the game itself rather than watching a game requires more concentration, which means being in full awareness and in that state, the ego is automatically dropped. While playing a game, if one is thinking about several different things, then the concentration is not complete and the game would be lost. When the concentration is 100%, then one exists as a mass of awareness, concentrating on only one single thing; being not aware of the body, the ego gets dropped and results in complete enjoyment of the game. Similarly, while reading a book, practicing music, enjoying a concert, painting, etc., when we immerse ourselves fully in any activity the ego gets dropped and we get to experience happiness by enjoying what we are doing.

So, the trick is to identify what we like and indulge in that activity fully with our complete unwavering attention, become free of the ego and be happy. If such activity happens to be our profession or our family relationship, then nothing like it. Unlike a movie or watching a game where the happiness lasts for only a few hours, enjoying the profession provides happiness until our retirement and enjoying the family relationships provides happiness till the very end.

For example, great sports stars like Roger Federer, Michael Jordan, Sachin Tendulkar, Christiano Ronaldo, etc., not only enjoy bringing their great performances into every single game but also when they do not have a game they enjoy practicing very hard for several hours every day. When you love your profession, work does not appear like work. Instead, the work becomes play and enables one to achieve great feats. It is the same with any professional, be it Edison or Einstein, Bill Gates or Steve Jobs. Doing what we love makes us get involved in it fully, which means being in full awareness during the activity. Being in full awareness automatically drops the ego resulting in enjoyment.

When work is enjoyed, then it is no more considered as work. Though engaged in action it seems like inaction. A mother pacifying her baby all night does not feel it like a big deal due to her selfless love. At the same time, some people consider the work as drudgery and eagerly wait for the Friday evening to relax and enjoy. So, when they venture out during the weekend to relax in a resort, beach, etc., they need to negotiate with the maddening traffic first to eventually find that all those places are fully crowded with people of similar thinking. Finally, when they return home on Sunday evening or Monday morning, instead of feeling relaxed, they find themselves more tired, exhausted and restless.

Bhagavad-Gita (4.18) says, *"One who sees inaction in action and action in inaction is intelligent among human beings"*. Ashtavakra-Gita (18.61) says, *"Even the inaction of a foolish man transforms itself into an activity and with the wise, even action results in the fruits of inaction"*.

To enjoy doing work and not have any kind of work-related stress *"either love your profession or make what you love as your profession"*. Increasing the skills, stamina and capabilities through constant practice, reading and watching videos related to our work would provide us the adequate ability to face bigger challenges. Once we have the confidence in our ability, then there is less anxiety and this enables us to actually enjoy the work-related challenges.

In all the above cases we used some external object such as movie, sports, thrilling activity, loveable profession, etc., to experience our happiness. During that duration when we are fully indulged in the activity with full concentration, we exist as a mass of Awareness, the ego gets dropped and hence the happiness results. To have the same happiness without the help of any external object, the direct method is meditation. Meditation is nothing but concentration. There are different forms of mediations practiced like listening to soothing music, guided meditation, breathing techniques, etc.

The most direct, simplest and effective meditation is the one advocated by Ramana Maharshi which we discussed earlier under the topic "Vastu". Just sit in a comfortable position, close the eyes and observe the breath. As the inhalation and exhalation are closely observed with unwavering concentration, silence is achieved easily. To quickly make the mind calm, silent and still, the breath observation is necessary. Once the mental silence is achieved, shift the concentration from breath and become aware of the silence. Once you are in the awareness of your silence, realize that it is your true nature. The silence is not you. The Awareness is you which is the Sentient Life Energy and its nature is silence. This is exactly the same silent state we experience in our deep sleep state.

In both the meditative and deep sleep states we are silent. The only difference is in this meditative silent state we are able to fully experience and take notice of our Silent Awareness. Once you are in full awareness of your silence, the ego is dropped and you can be free, feel liberated and be happy. Just like the nature of fire is heat, but heat is not fire, in the same way, the nature of Awareness is silence and the silence itself is not Awareness. "Being" and "Existing" as the Silent Awareness is the ultimate goal of the Vedic philosophy.

Silent Awareness

By constant attempt and practice, one can succeed in just being in **Silent Awareness** (Mundaka Upanishad 2.2.2–2.2.9). Just be. Be in the **Silent Awareness**. Be silent. Silent beatitude is the key. Being silent without doing any thinking is the goal. Exist as a thinker without doing any thinking. No mentation is necessary. Just be in Self-attention. Exist as a knower without trying to know anything in particular. Exist as a mass of **Silent Awareness** without trying to become aware of anything in particular. To help achieve the goal just watch your own silence with the fullest concentration. Enjoy your silence. Become aware of your silence.

Deliberately repeated the same thing using several different statements so that the readers can firmly grasp and realize, that is all there is to it. Brihad Aranyaka Upanishad (4.4.23) emphasizes the same. Enlightenment can be had here and now, at this very moment, says Ramana Maharshi. Being silent is our true nature. All the mental thoughts and verbal talks are disturbances happening on top of the underlying silence, just like the ripples are the disturbances on an otherwise calm and still lake. We disturb ourselves with the thoughts. All the thoughts and talks are happening because of the ego. Silent Awareness, Self, Atman is not a new entity that gets suddenly revealed. It has been always there but due to the incessant thoughts because of the ego the Self, Atman remains hidden.

Sadhu Om in his book "The Path of Sri Ramana" says, that so long our attention dwells on second and third persons (external objects) it is called 'mind' or 'intellect'. The attending is called kriya (doing) or karma (action). But on the other hand, as soon as the attention is fixed on the first person (or Self) and try to exist as a mass of Sentient Energy, mass of Awareness, it loses the names such as mind, intellect or ego sense. Therefore, the mind which attends to Self is no more the mind. The attention to Self is no longer a kriya (doing) or karma (action) or chintana (thinking). The Self-attention or being in the Silent Awareness is not of the nature of 'doing', rather it is of the nature of 'being' or 'existing'. This 'being' or 'existing' in Silent Awareness is our true nature.

Great illustrious Firebrand Acharya Sri Gaudapada, Shankaracharya's Guru's Guru, in his "Mandukya Karika (3.32)" says the same. When there are no desires and wants, the mind becomes free from the objects of cognition as there are no wants for the objects of cognition. Then he says in such a state, the mind ceases to be mind. In that state, the mind does not bring forth any more imaginations and fantasies due to the knowledge of the Truth which is 'being', 'existing' and 'experiencing' the Silent Awareness.

Once being in Silent Awareness for a few minutes is achieved, during that time one can experience the absence of the ego. After that one can achieve this state very easily without having to always close the eyes or meditate in a particular way. During sitting, standing, walking, bathing or practically anytime we are alone we can experience our Silent Awareness. We can be silent and observe that silence. Just be in the awareness of the silence. Once this state is experienced and realized, ego never bothers us again. This Silent Awareness state becomes our home.

Just like we do all our transactions at several places and finally get back to our home in the evening, in the same way, this state of being in Silent Awareness becomes our natural state. Whenever required to perform a duty, say as a father, as a spouse, as a professional, as a citizen, as a person, at that moment concentrate on whatever needs to be done and become silent again. When we make a business trip to another city, the first thing we do is to book a room in a hotel. Then we go and visit several different places in the city to do our business all day and finally we return to the comfort of the hotel room. In the same way, for whatever time we need to devote to do a particular activity or a duty, we should indulge in that fully and later we need to return to the comfort of being in Silent Awareness.

We all know that unpleasant things do happen in life which force us to think about them and that makes it difficult for us to be silent without any thoughts. D.V. Gundappa popularly known as DVG was a great 20th century philosopher and writer in Kannada language. His magnum opus is "Mankuthimmana Kagga" and the Wikipedia translates it as "Dull Thimma's Rigmarole". This work is treated as *"Kannada's Bhagavad-Gita"*. It is a collection of 945 poems, each being four lines in length and the subject matter is the same as what we are discussing here, which is dissolving our ego, nurturing noble thoughts, doing noble deeds, developing mental maturity and strength to abide in Silent Awareness. In that book, DVG says life is full of challenges, that's the way it is for everybody and we need to deal with those challenges by being solid and steady like a rock. Every test in our life makes us bitter or better. Every problem we face can make us or break us. The choice is ours, to choose to either become a victim or victorious.

While playing a game, we do not expect the opponent to make it easy for us so that we can win every point. Winning in such a manner would not make it exciting and enjoyable. We expect the opponent to make it as difficult as possible for us and we like to use our skills to overcome the challenges thrown at us and win the game. That's when the win is more satisfying and enjoyable. Sometimes a player gets hurt or injured during the game. The player endures the pain and continues the game or takes the time needed to recover from the injury and comes back to play the game again.

Life is a much bigger and real game and is full of challenges. We need to face the challenges and overcome them. The loss of loved ones, decline in business, setbacks in profession, unmet aspirations, etc., and the failures could be many. We are left with no other option but to face them, overcome them if possible, otherwise endure them. Let us cry when we have to. Let us endure the pain when we are forced to. The real pain and suffering actually happen due to continuous worrying. Even when there is no big tragedy or calamity, the mind engages in continuous thoughts because of the ego. Due to the ego, when the mind is engaged in ceaseless thoughts, becomes restless and agitated, we lose our happiness and forget our Silent Awareness (Mundaka Upanishad 3.1.1 - 3.1.2). When met with difficulty, after feeling down for some time we need to gather ourselves up and become ready to face the next set of challenges that life is going to throw at us just like an injured player who becomes ready after recovering from the injury.

Being in the Silent Awareness is also called as being in the present or being in the "Now". It is not that we should not plan for the future or learn from the past. Continuous thinking about the past or the future needs to be avoided. It is the ego which keeps the mind engaged in constant thinking. An inspirational quote says, *"Never think hard about the past.*

It brings tears… Don't think more about the future. It brings fears… Live this present moment with a smile. It brings cheers".

Ego – The Evil Devil

Whenever we are alone if we cannot enjoy being in **Silent Awareness** which is observing our own silence, then the ego takes over and gives rise to various thoughts. The ego makes the feeling of "I" prominent and starts generating thoughts about the past or the future. The ego makes us fantasize with futuristic thoughts and there is always an element of fear and anxiety as there is always the chance of those fantasies not materializing. The past which is dead and gone and nothing can be done to correct it, the ego likes to brood over it. Bringing that long gone past incident into the present memory the ego makes us sulk, cry for revenge, crave to avenge and become emotive. Thus, the ego makes us get agitated in the present, thinking about something that happened in the past.

It is the ego which discriminates as "us" and "them" (Brihad Aranyaka Upanishad 4.3.31) and in the name of religion, sect, language, nationality, etc., provokes hatred and animosity in "us" towards "them". Sarvagna, a 16th century Kannada poet says, *"We walk on the same earth. We drink the same water. We use the same fire. Then why discriminate amongst ourselves as 'us' and 'them' using the man-made artificial concepts such as caste, creed, religion, nationality, etc.".* In some cases, the ego makes us compare "us" with "them", feel worthless and get into depression. All these prove that *"Idle mind is the devil's workshop"* and the devil is our own ego.

It helps to understand this evil ego a little better because this ego is the veil over our true Self. The ego hides our real nature which is to be silent all the time by projecting various thoughts, wants, desires, etc., in our minds. Our poor mind is not the culprit. It is the ego which is the real culprit (Maha Upanishad 3.16–3.21). Ego does not signify pride. Ego is actually "Aham Vritti" (I-ness, I-thought) which makes us say I am male, my age is so and so, this property is mine, I am the owner of this pen, etc.

Because of the ego, the thoughts are always centered about "I". I want this, I do not want that. I like this, I do not like that.

If we observe a little bit more deeply into this ego some more ugly facts emerge. Let us say I go to a nice expensive fine dining place with exquisite ambience. After enjoying the great delectable food, my ego says tomorrow in the office during the tea break I could boast about the experience in front of my colleagues. Having enjoyed the great food, one could keep quiet. This ego projects highly imaginative false things that by boasting one could feel good. Let us say somebody else had enjoyed great food and is bragging in front of me, then his ego is gloating and my ego is sulking with jealousy and envy that I did not get such an opportunity and my budget would not allow me to visit such an expensive dining place.

This ego holds us under such a grip that it makes us indulge in really dirty deeds. Boasting, showing off, wanting to teach somebody a lesson, wanting to prove a point, one-upmanship, trying to rub somebody's nose on the floor, wanting to avenge an insult, wanting to possess more than others, wanting to forcibly convert others and make them accept my point of view, my sect or my religion, wanting to act big, expecting others to treat me big, wanting others to appreciate and the list goes on. None of these are really necessary; they strew venom around, spread hatred and distress to others and finally trouble our mind immensely by making it engage in ceaseless meaningless thoughts.

Take the case of expecting appreciation from others. Today where are Pete Sampras, Boris Becker, John McEnroe, Bjorn Borg, etc.? At that time every one appreciated their game and their shots in every game. Nobody talks much about them now. Does that mean what they did was not great? Definitely what they did was great, what they achieved were great feats, they were a treat to watch and possessed great talent. Now comes the real understanding. Though other people might have stopped appreciating them now, they would not have stopped appreciating themselves for what they achieved. They would very vividly remember their every single achievement. Several great moments they might have had on the tennis court would still remain green in their memories. Thus, our own appreciation and delighting at our own accomplishment is more important, permanent and nobody else need to know about them. Even if others come to know about our accomplishment, their praise or insult should not affect us at all. Let us welcome the reviews and criticisms. But let us not let our ego to fool us and guide us to be in constant expectation of seeking others approval and appreciation.

Analyzing the ego to this gory detail, we can see its ugliness and venom. According to the expert mythologist Dr. Devdutt Pattanaik, in ancient Indian mythology, this ego is symbolically mentioned as "Haalahala Visha" (potent poison). Everybody's ego is the same and equally venomous and harmful. Hitler, Mussolini, Idi Amin, Saddam Hussain and all other tyrants put together cannot match the evilness of the ego. We need to be extremely wary of our own ego and develop utter disgust towards it.

Developing this kind of attitude towards our own ego, understanding its ugliness and venomous potency helps reduce our thoughts and realize our own Silent Awareness which is our true Self. Dropping the ego helps us to become free from the clutches of desires. Once free of desires then our true Self, Atman gets revealed, says Brihad Aranyaka Upanishad (4.4.6–4.4.7).

Reducing the Ego

The ego is the impurity covering our true Self just in the same way, moss hides the pure water. Just drag the moss, set it aside and the pure water reveals itself. In the same way, our pure nature is covered by the impurities due to the ego. Step by step we need to move towards reducing the ego and attaining the mental purity by doing noble things, thinking good thoughts and always talking good and kind words. Otherwise, it is impossible to realize the **Silent Awareness** if we have even a little bit of selfishness or self-centered thoughts due to the ego (Mundaka Upanishad 3.1.8).

Swami Ranganathananda beautifully describes selflessness by saying, *"When I close my eyes, I experience the Peace within. When I open my eyes,*

I want to say what can I do for you?". However, if the ego is present, then exactly the opposite happens. When I close my eyes, due to the selfish ego I get all kinds of thoughts, desires, likes, dislikes and the mind becomes completely restless. Then when I open my eyes, again due to selfishness, I would think about what I can get from you.

We need to reduce the ego by doing good deeds and nurturing good thoughts. There are seven virtues mentioned in the Bible which are prudence (wisdom), justice (righteousness), temperance (moderation), courage (fortitude), faith, hope and charity. These need not be practiced only by Christians; in fact, everyone can practice them and they help reduce one's ego. Similarly, one should be highly wary of the Arishadvargas (band of six enemies) and Pancha Kleshas (five afflictions of the mind). The Golden Rule should be followed which says, *"Treat others as one would wish to be treated"*. The virtues present in the Ten Commandments could be practiced by everybody. It says do not murder, do not commit adultery, do not steal, do not utter lies and do not covet. All the religions in the world preach that virtues are paramount and essential to be considered as a human being.

Thiruvalluvar, a great Tamil poet who lived during 300 BCE says, *"For people who harm, you do so much great good to them so that they feel ashamed and realize their mistakes"*. The American civil rights activist Martin Luther King echoes the same by saying, *"Darkness cannot drive out darkness; only light can do that. Hate cannot drive out hate; only love can do that"*.

Basically, all the good qualities and virtues help purify the mind. A pure mind is highly essential to experience the Silent Awareness (Kaivalya Upanishad 1.4). Not practicing the good virtues makes the mind impure, the ego becomes extremely strong and makes the mind restless and highly agitated with endless desires and ceaseless thoughts. When the ego becomes strong, it results in I know it all, who are others to teach me? People do not know how big I am, etc. We already analyzed the complete ugliness of the ego. The more the ego, lesser the happiness and farther we are from the Silent Awareness, the true Self. One should develop the aversion towards one's own ego, its ugly ways and imaginary hallucinations by analyzing the egoistic, self-centered thoughts.

The very first step towards mental purity is to learn to say "Enough". There are people richer than us and there are people who are less fortunate than us. Understanding this clearly, we need to be thankful for what we have, learn to live a contented life by saying "Enough". Popular American singer Alison Maria Krauss says, *"I don't look for bliss, just contentment"*. It is not that one should not have ambition and one should not prosper. It is enjoying fully with all the enjoyments provided by our own abilities and capabilities. Let us attend to our needs by all means. But let us not attend to our greed. Everything we use for our needs like the bed, food, clothes, shelter, pens, books, watches, etc., let us ensure that they are of good quality and provide best possible comfort. Let them be within our budget and let them be only for us and not to show-off.

We need to nurture good thoughts. For example, when we buy our vegetables, we need to give a moment to think about the number of people who have sweated and toiled just to provide us with food. The farmers sweat in the farm, the transporters transport far and wide across the nation, the distributors and finally the people in the retail outlet, all have to work to make the vegetables available to us. Though we are paying, still if these many people were not there, our money would be useless. We should clearly understand that these whole set of people belonging to different religions, different races, speak different languages, have different nationalities, etc. The car we use, the bed we sleep on, the refrigerator, the phone, every single thing that provides us comfort, comes from the society where a whole lot of people are working tirelessly round the year to make each one us have a comfortable living. Thus, everyone irrespective of caste or creed is working for the betterment of humanity as a whole. Then, thinking as an individual, I would think let there be my little contribution too for this great cause. Instead of saying "Thank God it is Friday", I would cheerfully start saying "Thank God it is Monday" and be self-motivated to go to work brimming with enthusiasm.

With these kinds of thoughts, suddenly the whole outlook towards the world changes. The "Dignity of Labor" gets established automatically. The prevailing capitalistic Profit Mentality makes way for the sacred Service Mentality. If I am a bus driver, I would understand that the entire busload of people I am ferrying are doing different kinds of work that are required by the society which includes me too. Then I would drive the bus not just with care, but also with a lot of love just like the way I would drive my car while travelling with my own family members. Treating the entire world as one big family is the concept advocated by Vedic philosophy and is called "Vasudhaiva Kutumbakam". This Sanskrit phrase appears in Maha Upanishad (6.71–6.75). It says, *"One is a relative, the other stranger, say the small minded. The entire world is a family, live the magnanimous".*

Dropping the ego means dropping the first person thought. When 'I' itself is not there where is the question of 'you' and 'them' which are the second and third person thoughts. That means when I do not give importance to my ego then I am not affected by anything around me and I always feel comfortable, contented and happy. In other words, when I do not give importance to my own caste or creed then naturally I would not be interested in what religion people around me belong to. I just treat others as human beings just like me and become completely insensitive to the cast, creed, race, religion and nationality of others. I would start seeing oneness in everybody and recognize everyone including me as one Sentient Life Energy.

The one big clarion call given by Vedanta is "Drop the ego". You can love your Jesus and the Pope, you can love your Allah and his Prophet, you can love your Krishna and the Gurus. There is no need to change one's God or religion. The Vedic philosophy says just *"surrender to the God you love"* completely. Can there be any greater secular philosophy than this? The Vedantic message *"Drop the ego",* is to everybody irrespective of one's religion and it applies equally to atheists too.

Doing true Bhakti (devotion) to the God one loves and completely surrendering to that God helps to drop the ego. Complete surrender is a sine-qua-non, one should love the God truly and intensely, should try to be always in the thought of God and should not be interested in any other selfish thoughts when not engaged in any activity. In the case of an atheist, rationalist, naturalist, scientist, etc., whenever alone or not doing any work one should try to be in the Silent Awareness which helps to drop the ego. The end result is the same, which is dropping the ego. Wholeheartedly dedicated devotion to God and living with only Godly thoughts is Bhakti Yoga (path of devotion). Gaining the knowledge and after understanding clearly, being in Silent Awareness is Jnana Yoga (path of knowledge).

Global Peace – Attainable Goal

What's the point in going through all this, understanding it, dropping the ego and being with our **Silent Awareness**? The point is to first attain Individual Peace and then try to materialize and realize World Peace. We saw how Nature is also trying to give the same message in our Sushupti (deep sleep state). We always experience and enjoy the peace and happiness we get in deep sleep. So, to have individual peace, drop the ego which is what happens in the Sushupti. We also saw how in the deep sleep state we all become one. There is no religion, no nationality, no sect, nothing in the deep sleep. Nature is showing us how we can all become one and establish World Peace by just dropping our individual egos.

Earlier Germans had divided themselves into East and West. After the Berlin Wall was torn down, the difference ceased to exist and now they are one happy Germans. If we learn to stop differentiating as "us" and "them" by dropping our egos then a golden age will arrive where every single nation in the world would be able to tear down the imaginary fences and needless walls built around their borders and live harmoniously as one single humanity (Brihad Aranyaka Upanishad, 4.3.32).

Science has made significant advancements to benefit the mankind. Large computers have shrunk to tablets and pocket-sized smartphones. 3-D printing is becoming a reality. We are inching closer towards self-driven, driverless automobiles. The Internet has made the entire world into a small, well connected global village. Internet of Things (IOT) is around the corner. The stupendous advancements in medicine are saving innumerous human lives around the world. All the progress science has made in various fields such as space, energy, transportation, etc., have all been for the betterment of the mankind. Unfortunately, it is also the same science that is responsible for AK-47s, battle tanks, battleships, nuclear submarines, B-12 bombers, laser-guided missiles, atomic and hydrogen bombs. All the countries in the world are on the edge whenever any of the countries possessing the nuclear and hydrogen bombs indulges in saber-rattling. Testing the missiles make people in neighboring countries live in a state of fear. Firing the missiles make people live in a state of hunger, pain and unimaginable suffering.

Violence should be shunned completely. Violence cannot be justified under any pretext whether it is for the caste, creed, sect, religion, nation or any other reason. Dropping the ego allows us to drop the discrimination amongst us. Despite having been endowed with intellect, not using it wisely and engaging in violence is silly and absurd. This is what Jonathan Swift in his classic "Gulliver's Travels" tries to convey by weaving a story about Lilliputians who had divided themselves into little-endians and big-endians. Lilliputians are a race of tiny people who are less than 6 inches tall. All Lilliputians traditionally used to break their eggs on the larger ends. Once the prince cut his hand while breaking an egg at the traditional larger end and hence the emperor decreed that henceforth all the eggs be broken only on the smaller end. However, several Lilliputians opposed to change their traditional habit and hence their race got divided into two and they lost peace completely, quarreled and waged wars for generations. Through this satire, Jonathan Swift is trying to convey that no matter whatever be the reason, if we engage in wars and violence, the reasons always look flimsy and we would look as silly as the quarrelling bird-brained Lilliputians.

There is only one electrical energy and there cannot be two different electrical energies. In the same way, there cannot be two different life energies. There is only one Universal Sentient Life Energy. Various instruments like bulb, fan, TV, etc., differ in their name and form but are powered by the same electrical energy. In the same way, all of us differ in our name and form but are powered and provided life by one single Sentient Life Energy.

If we cognize the life energy as a thread, then all of us are individual beads of pearls strung on the same single thread uniting this entire world into one single beautiful necklace (Bhagavad-Gita 7.7). Different colored and shaped beads lend beauty to the necklace. In the same way, we should not see differences due to our different cultures, languages, nationality, race, religion and all other diversities but understand that these diversities actually enrich the splendor and grandeur of the magnificent planet we live in. All of us should stop identifying ourselves as individual beads and instead, identify ourselves with the resplendent thread, the underlying substratum uniting us into one single dazzling necklace. Instead of identifying ourselves with our bodies we need to identify ourselves with the Sentient Life Energy which is the transcendent substratum uniting all of us.

If only Science and Scientists were to realize the message given by Nature in our deep sleep experience, then human misery could be eradicated entirely. Every single tear from every human eye can be wiped off. In deep sleep, we experience Peace, Oneness and Unity in Diversity because we are forced to drop the ego.

We have analyzed in detail how to drop the ego deliberately in our waking state, be in Silent Awareness and experience the Peace, Oneness and Unity in Diversity. If this can be clearly understood, then everyone could come together to make a great universal revolution, the enormity and cause of which the world has never witnessed before. Such a revolution would be mammoth as it would sweep the entire world and not be confined to any single nation. The cause or the goal of the revolution would be to establish blissful *Individual Peace* and briskly march towards ushering in the glorious *World Peace*. That is the ultimate success mankind as a whole is definitely capable of achieving.

Now it is "Every Human Being's Burden" to blast open the floodgates of the heart filled with Oneness and Happiness and allow them to lovingly gush and engulf the entire humanity. Fondly taking a bow to the great "King of Pop" who gave unparalleled immense joy to all of us, let us recognize that *it is time to start with the man in the mirror asking him to change his ways if we want to make the world a better place*.

Chapter 3
Sadhana

"Continuous effort - not strength or intelligence – is the key to unlocking our potential"

– Winston Churchill

SUCCESS IS RESULT OF PASSIONATE EFFORT

❧ ❧ ❧

Om Puurnam-Adah Puurnam-Idam Puurnaat-Puurnam-Udacyate
Puurnasya Puurnam-Aadaaya Puurnam-Eva-Avashishyate
Om Shaanti Shaanti Shaantihi

Om, That (outer world) is complete and infinite.
This (inner world) is complete and infinite.
If infinity is removed (subtracted) from infinity, what remains is
only infinity.
Om, Peace, Peace, Peace.

❧ ❧ ❧

Sadhana - Effort

"We all have dreams. But in order to make dreams come into reality, it takes an awful lot of determination, dedication, self-discipline, and effort."

– Jesse Owens

Sadhana (effort) means relentless effort, patient endurance, determined persistence, dogged perseverance, staunch endeavor and resolute struggle to achieve the desired goal. Nothing worth having was ever achieved without the effort. The enormity of the task, the challenge of getting it done, the hardships along the way, everything fades away into darkness when the brilliant light of passion is shone upon it. Steve Prefontaine, a popular American long-distance runner of the early seventies, said: *"To give anything less than your best is to sacrifice the gift"*.

Vedanta not only urges us to put in the required effort but also shows and guides us as to how to channelize and make a focused effort that is guaranteed to succeed. Vedic philosophy shows the path that can be followed by any sincere seeker belonging to any religion to achieve the ultimate goal which is dropping the ego and always remaining in the thought of one's beloved God or just abiding in the **Silent Awareness**. The exact same path shown by Vedanta can be very well followed by anybody to achieve any other goal such as to succeed in profession, business, education, sports or any other field.

In the "Blissful Life" chart Sadhana is the outer rectangle and should be traversed in the anticlockwise direction starting from the Guru. In the chart, after a complete rotation, one comes back to the Guru again. It means one should again seek further knowledge from the Guru, gain much more precise understanding than before and tread the path again, which is practicing and putting into action whatever knowledge that has been understood. This effort is called Sadhana and the person putting the effort is called Sadhaka. One will have to traverse the path multiple times, each time gaining more knowledge from the same Guru or different Guru and each time further intensifying the effort required to achieve the goal.

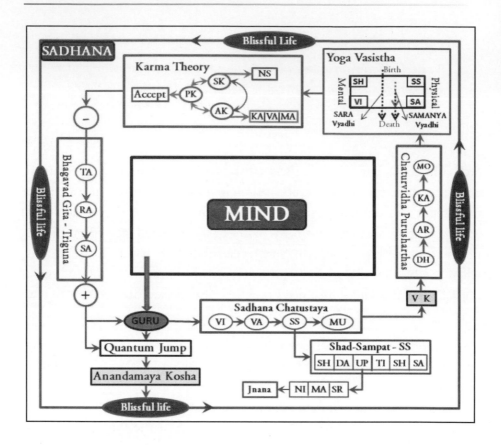

Guru - Teacher

Guru is a Sanskrit term that connotes someone who is a teacher, counselor, inspirer, guide, expert or master of certain Jnana (Knowledge) or Field. The Guru is given colossal importance in the ancient Vedic texts. Dvaya Upanishad (1.4) says, "Gu" means darkness, "Ru" means resistance and hence "Guru" means a person who resists the darkness of ignorance. A hymn of Rig Veda describes Guru as the source and inspirer of the Knowledge for the one who seeks. Chandogya Upanishad proclaims that it is only through Guru that one attains Knowledge. Katha Upanishad declares Guru as indispensable to the acquisition of Knowledge. Taittiriya Upanishad describes human knowledge as that which connects the teacher and the student through the medium of exposition. Svetasvatara Upanishad goes still further and equates the need of reverence and devotion to the Guru to be the same as for the God.

Guru with his immense wisdom, enormous love and abundant patience shows the path of light (of knowledge) to dispel the darkness (of ignorance). Guru can be a person, scriptures, books, commentaries, discourses, audio and video lectures. Guru can only show the path, but still, it is the student who has to tread the path after gaining a clear understanding of the knowledge.

Sadhana Chatushtaya

Sadhana Chatushtaya means Fourfold Qualification described by the great Vedic Guru Sri Adi Shankara who lived in India for only 32 years in the early part of the 8th century. He crisscrossed the entire country several times educating the people all along his path on Vedic philosophy and established four mutts (Vedic Shrines) in four corners of the country. The sheer amount of the monumental work done by Shankaracharya within his short lifespan shows that he could not have slept for more than 3-4 hours every day. It brings tears to our eyes and makes us bow our head in reverence when we think about the painstaking stupendous efforts of Shankara, not for his personal benefit but for the benefit of the entire humankind to realize the *Individual Peace* first and then gallop towards attaining and establishing the *World Peace*.

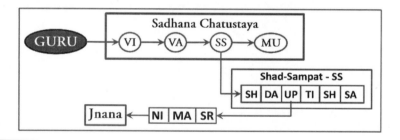

Sadhana Chatushtaya, the fourfold qualifications are **VI**veka (reasoning), **VA**iragya (dispassion), **S**had **S**ampat (treasure of six virtues) and **MU**mukshutva (burning desire to attain the goal). Intense Sadhana (effort) is required to attain these fourfold qualifications to become eligible to attain the desired goal.

After fervent practice, one would gain the wisdom and start operating more using Vignanamaya Kosha (intellectual sheath) instead of depending more on Manomaya Kosha (mental sheath). As one starts depending more on the intellect, one becomes calm and collected, rational, does not get irritated easily and there are no kneejerk reactions.

Viveka - Power of Discrimination

Viveka (VI) is the intellectual ability to discriminate or discern between the truth and the untruth (Satya and Asatya), permanent and the impermanent (Nitya and Anithya), Self and the non-Self (Atman and Anatman).

Viveka means reasoning and comprehending using the intellect. The previous chapter was dedicated to the topic "Viveka" where we explored different reasonings to detect and grasp the Sentient Energy which is being in the Silent Awareness. In this section, we shall see a new and different reasoning explicated in "Aparoksha Anubhuti" meaning "Direct Experience" authored by Adi Shankaracharya.

We usually identify ourselves with our body and we even point to our body and say this is "I". Shankara renders robust arguments to show that we are actually the Sentient Energy and the body is only an instrument powered by that Sentient Energy which is the Chit Shakti or Self or Consciousness or Awareness or Atman.

Ekam Anekam Viveka - One and Many

We clearly feel that the feeling "I" points to "**one**" complete individual which is us. "I" always means singular, not plural. But the body is clearly made of many different parts such as fingers, hands, legs, foot, eyes, ears, heart, lungs, liver, kidneys, etc. Each body part is different and the body is an assembly of "**many**" different parts. How can one and many become the same? Therefore, Shankara thunders that there cannot be any greater ignorance than not recognizing "I" as the **One** Sentient Energy and instead, mistaking the one "I" to be the body which is clearly made up of **Many** different parts.

Nitya Anitya Viveka - Eternal and Ephemeral

Ever since we can remember, the feeling of "I" has never changed. The Sentient Energy inside us has been the same ever since we were born.

Clearly, the body has been constantly changing, hence it is ephemeral. All of us clearly know that we have different bodies at different stages of our lives such as infant, toddler, child, teen, youth, middle-aged, elderly and old. How can the eternal and ephemeral be the same? Therefore, there cannot be any greater ignorance than not recognizing "I" as the unchanging **Eternal** Sentient Energy and instead, mistaking "I" to be the ever-changing, temporary, **Ephemeral** body.

Anthar Bahya Viveka – Inside and Outside

When we wear a shirt, clearly the shirt is outside the body and the body is inside the shirt. That means what is inside and what is outside are two distinct things and can never be the same. We clearly feel that the feeling of "I" comes from inside whereas the body is outside. How can inside and outside be the same? Therefore, there cannot be any greater ignorance than not recognizing "I" as the Sentient Energy which is the controller present **Inside** and instead, mistaking "I" to be the body which is the controlled and is **Outside**.

Chit Jada Viveka – Sentient and Insentient

When we look at our hand, we are looking at the hand and it is not that the hand is looking at us. That means we are the Sentient Energy which is the Consciousness or Awareness. The hand or any body part is inert and insentient. How can the sentient and the insentient be the same? Therefore, there cannot be any greater ignorance than not recognizing "I" as the **Sentient** Energy and instead, mistaking "I" to be the **Insentient** body.

Shankara says without doing such enquiry and reasoning, an ignorant person though uses language like "My body", "This body is mine", yet remains deluded and thinks "I am the body". Shankara argues that when we say "My car", I am the owner and the car is the owned. The owner and the owned are two distinct things and can never be the same. We use language like "My body", "My mind", "My intellect", and hence we cannot be the body or mind or intellect. We are actually the Sentient Energy which is the true owner powering the body, the mind and the intellect.

Then Shankara simply sizzles in trying to make us understand the true nature of our own Self, the Sentient Energy, the real "I". "I" am Nirvikara (changeless), Nirakara (formless), Avyaya (undecaying), Niramaya (without any diseases, only the body gets diseases), Nirabhasa (without any appearance), Nirvikalpa (without any modifications), Nirguna (without any qualities), Nitya (eternal), Nirmala (stainless), Nishchala (immobile), Anantha (endless), Ajara (ageless), Amara (deathless).

If we carefully observe, all the above description fits the description of any energy, be it electrical energy, magnetic, heat, light, etc. Every single word is applicable to any energy. The Self, the real "I" is also an energy, the Chit Shakti that is powering all the organs in the body. Unlike all other energies which are inert, this life energy within us is Sentient and we can very much experience it by dropping our ego and being in Silent Awareness.

Vedic texts also contain some descriptions that are applicable only to the Sentient Energy within us and do not apply to any other energy. The nature of the Sentient Energy, the Self, is said to be Satchidananda (Tejo Bindu Upanishad 3.11) which is Sat (Existence) (Chandogya Upanishad 6.2.1), Chit (Consciousness) (Aitareya Upanishad 3.1.3) and Ananda (Bliss) (Taittiriya Upanishad 3.6.1). Sat (Existence) means the Sentient Energy exists in the same manner in the past, the present and the future without any change. Chit (Consciousness) implies Sentience and that's why we are calling it as Sentient Life Energy. Ananda (Bliss) is the nature of the Life Energy which can be experienced with a quiet mind and being in Silent Awareness.

Explaining further the Vedic texts describe the Self, the Sentient Energy as Ekam (one), Ekam Eva Advithiyam (one and only one without a second), Shantham (peaceful), Swayam Prakasha (self-luminous or self-effulgent), Prajna (Consciousness or Awareness), Jnatha (knower),

Sakshi (witness), Agrahya (ungraspable), Anirvachaniya (ineffable), Shabdha Vivarjita (beyond words), Sukshmani (subtlest of the subtle).

Viveka, the reasoning is very much needed to first understand the concept clearly without any doubt before starting the execution. In the software world, we say do the design first before touching the keyboard and writing a single line of code. There may be refinements in the design as we indulge in the effort, but right in the beginning having a concrete design and meticulous planning are essential to succeed in achieving any goal. Such kind of total commitment, dedicated involvement and attention to the minute detail bring out the passion. The passion, in turn, brings out the best effort, makes the effort enjoyable and enables one to achieve great feats with ease, grace and elegance.

A passionate architect thinks about the structure or the building while sitting, standing, walking or bathing. Such an architect would be able to imagine and clearly visualize the structure from all the 360-degree angles even before a single brick or a piece of iron is moved to the site.

This is exactly what is Viveka (reasoning), which is, doing the required reasoning and clearly understanding the job to be done before embarking on getting the job done.

Vairagya - Dispassion

One who has Viveka (discriminative wisdom) cannot fail to have Vairagya (dispassion) as they are interdependent. It is nothing but renunciation of all momentary enjoyments and instant gratifications. With the power of Viveka, Vairagya can be explained in simple sentences in three levels.

First level → "Whatever I have, I have it, whatever I don't have, I don't have."

Second level → "If I have something, so what, if I don't have something, so what."

Third level → "If I have something or if I don't have something it's of no consequence, the most important thing is how much I am happy at any given moment."

Basically, it is not gloating over something we have and not desperately craving for something which we do not have. Both are achieved by dropping the ego. Viveka (reasoning) and Vairagya (dispassion) help us to drop the ego.

We already saw how continuously eating even at a great dining place becomes nauseating. Continuously relaxing at a great luxurious resort also becomes boring. Continuously travelling around the world visiting various tourist locations becomes tiring. Vedic texts say that the purpose of everything present in this world is for us to realize their temporariness, momentariness and impermanence.

Many of the eastern philosophies state "Life is full of suffering". This is often totally misunderstood as that eastern thinking considers the human life as miserable, full of suffering, worthless and hence it is immaterial whether life is there or not. What the statement actually means is explained in the previous paragraph. It is understanding the truth that everything the world has to offer provides only temporary enjoyment. One who does not use the intellect, does not understand the temporariness of worldly pleasures, pretends that one could escape disease, old age and death due to the wealth, intelligence, technology, comfort and luxuries, keeps indulging in sense gratifications, never satisfied and ever in need of something with endless desires, whose thoughts are always self-centered is actually considered to be in the state of suffering.

Poverty, dimwit, handicap, disease, etc., are not considered suffering, it is misfortune. Through the famous poem "Bhaja Govindam", Shankara conveys that the tendency of human being to not understand the truth despite being endowed with intellect and ignorantly clinging on to temporary worldly pleasures and shackled by self-centered thoughts till the very end until the life gets snatched abruptly by death is considered as bondage and suffering.

Does that mean we should not enjoy with what the world has to offer? No. Vedanta is not saying that we should never enjoy. It is asking us to understand the temporary, fleeting nature of everything and just take it easy to avoid endless mental agitation, excessive exertion and extreme exhaustion.

Swami Vivekananda concurs by saying, "*Fulfill your desire for power and everything else, and after you have fulfilled the desire, will come the time when you will know that they are all very little things; but until you have fulfilled this desire, until you have passed through that activity, it is impossible for you to come to the state of calmness, serenity, and self-surrender*".

Interestingly this is exactly what Socrates says, "*The unexamined life is not worth living*", urging us to indulge in the worldly things so that we can have a deep comprehension of the world, clearly understand and realize the transient and momentary happiness they provide. It was the same poverty-stricken Socrates while striding through the city's busy central marketplace, looking at the mass of several things for sale, he would harrumph provocatively, "*How many things I have no need of!*" That's the sign of the wise who have developed Vairagya (dispassion).

Shankara says a sincere seeker practicing Vairagya should develop an indifference to the worldly things just like the kind of indifference we show to the excreta of a crow. On another occasion, Shankara says the seeker should develop utter dispassion, distaste and disgust for the momentary happiness provided by the sense organs, just like the disgust we have towards vomited food.

The same Vairagya fiercely advised by Shankara can be followed to succeed in the one's profession also. What it means is that apart from the current project or the venture we are interested in, we should develop the same outright dispassion and distaste towards all the things that are unrelated to our goal. We should attend to only the necessary duties and at all other times be contemplating or working on the project. Vairagya means any distraction should be found irritating, any diversion of time and resource should be frowned upon, develop a prodigious appetite to succeed and stoke the fire in the belly to put in the unflinching relentless effort towards attaining the desired goal.

Shad Sampat - Six Virtues

Shad means six, Sampat means treasure. **Shad Sampat** (SS) means the six treasures which the seeker should try to amass. The six treasures are **SH**ama (calmness), **DA**ma (self-control), **UP**arati (withdrawal), **TI**tiksha (forbearance), **SH**raddha (faith) and **SA**madhana (focus).

We can classify these six qualities as three pairs and in each pair one quality is internal and the other is external. Internal means how we should be feeling within ourselves and external means how we need to interact with the external world.

Shama and Dama

Shama (tranquility) is the inner silence, calmness and firm control over the mind. The mind has a built-in tendency to run out wantonly attracted by external objects. Using Viveka (reasoning) we need to continually observe and ponder over the transient, temporary and fleeting happiness provided by the external objects for the amount of effort exerted and the energy expended. Shama is not suppression; it is training the mind with the clear understanding of Viveka, reigning over the desires by practicing Vairagya (dispassion) and hammering down the ego to be relieved from ceaseless thoughts, worries, pain and suffering.

Dama (self-control) means control over the sense organs such as the eyes. For the one who is well established in Shama (calmness) and has gained control over the mind and control over the senses, Dama comes naturally. Sometimes when one loses control over the mind, yet retains control over the sense organs that is called Dama.

For example, one may get angry, but refraining from using harsh words is Dama. A desire may arise to eat sweets, yet if one controls the legs from walking towards that sweet, restrains the hands from picking up the sweet and successfully forbids the tongue from tasting the sweet, it is called Dama.

Shama is the internal restraint of the mind (desires) and Dama is the external restraint of the sense organs (actions). If the mind is well controlled by practicing the Shama, then Dama comes naturally. But consciously practicing Dama makes the control of the mind much easier.

Uparati and Titiksha

Uparati (withdrawal) is the state of satiety. It is turning the mind resolutely away from temporary enjoyments. This state of mind comes naturally when one has shrewdly practiced Viveka (reasoning), Vairagya (dispassion), Shama (tranquil mind) and Dama (control of sense organs). The best Uparati is that condition of the mind where the thoughts are free from the influence of external objects.

Uparati becomes intense when the mind is always engaged in SHravana (listening), MAnana (remembering) and NIdhidhyasana (enquiry, contemplation and realization). All the three have to be repeated as many times as required until the concept is clearly grasped and the realization is experienced. This is called Jnana (knowledge).

- Shravana is listening to a teacher or reading a book. Simply reading or listening without understanding is unproductive. Doubts should be cleared by talking to the teacher or another expert or searching and reading other articles or books.

- Manana is remembering and recollecting what has been learnt during Shravana. Manana reveals the gaps if present in our understanding so that one can make attempts to clear those doubts and close those gaps.

- Nidhidhyasana is the firm grasping of the concept without any doubt and experiencing it.

This is precisely what one does to learn a concept thoroughly. For example, to understand a mathematical theorem, one has to first study or listen to the teacher. Then one has to recollect and reflect upon it. If any doubt remains then one has to re-read and try to improve the understanding. Once understood, then one can remain established in the truth of the knowledge gained.

Titiksha (forbearance) is the tolerance to face any challenges and endurance under any circumstances. We need to act according to the challenge thrown at us and try to overcome it. Sometimes we are unable to thwart the pain or loss. In such cases, we need to firmly and calmly endure without becoming restless and agitated and without feeling miserable and devastated.

For example, if we are pricked by a thorn, it definitely hurts. We just remove the thorn, throw it away and forget about it. But if it is a bigger thorn then even after the thorn is removed the pain could last for a few days. We have no choice but to endure the pain. It is foolish to curse the thorn or Nature, boorish to vent the anger on anybody around us and childish to let the mind get agitated.

The ego selfishly desires to be comfortable at all times and this is the height of folly. Can there be light alone without darkness? Victory alone without defeat? Roses alone without thorns? Gain alone without loss? Pleasure alone without pain? Success alone without failure?

Swami Tejomayananda says that when one travels in a vehicle with good shock absorbers, the ride is smooth even if the road is bad. Titiksha (endurance) is the shock absorber with which one rides the patches of rough terrain of life without sacrificing one's enthusiasm.

In sports, the opponent throws many challenges and tries to make it difficult for us to win the game. Life is a much bigger game and we need to be always ready to face any amount of challenges and difficulties that come our way. The Kannada poet DVG (D. V. Gundappa), in his masterpiece "Manku Thimmana Kagga" (Dull Thimma's Rigmarole) regarding endurance, says, "*Be solid like a rock amidst the torrential rains of difficulties that fate might pour upon us*". In another place, DVG says, "*Zip your lips and valiantly endure your difficulties*".

Shraddha and Samadhana

Shraddha (Faith) is the intense faith in what one has learnt based on one's own reasoning, understanding and experience. Shraddha is not blind faith. Instead, it is the everlasting unshakeable faith obtained due to the clear comprehension of the knowledge gained. This steadfast faith propels one to tread the path shown by the knowledge with dedication, determination, devotion and conviction along with an avid zeal to achieve the goal.

Samadhana (focus) is the single-pointedness of the mind. Samadhana also means peace obtained by perfect concentration, firm anchoring of the mind, establishing the mental stability, peaceful inner composure and graceful poise. Samadhana is not halfhearted indulgence due to curiosity but the unwavering concentration, sharp focus and wholehearted commitment to achieve the desired goal. A sincere seeker constantly contemplates on the Sentient Energy with total concentration without giving way to any other thought. A successful professional contemplates on the problem at hand with total concentration without being distracted by any other thing.

Mumukshutva – Burning Desire

Mumukshutva (MU) is the burning desire, intense longing and passionate yearning to achieve the desired goal. It is about staying focused and keep on moving towards the goal, all the time enjoying the journey. It is all about dreaming big, being intensely passionate about it, having a fierce drive to achieve, preparedness to work hard and not giving up under any situation. This is what Vedanta advises the seeker, which is to dream big and have the highest goal which is seeking the ultimate Truth. The same advice is very much applicable to anybody to think big and achieve any desired goal in any other field as well.

Sadhana Chatushtaya Summary

Acquiring the four-fold qualifications (Sadhana Chatushtaya) makes the mind calm and to interact with the world one would start relying more on Vignanamaya Kosha (VK), the intellectual sheath.

The first qualification, the Viveka (reasoning) is acquired by doing the Vichara (enquiry) to learn and understand the concept clearly.

Then comes Vairagya (dispassion) which is being utterly disinterested in anything that is unrelated to the goal.

The six-fold wealth (Shad Sampat) are controlling the mind (Shama), controlling of the senses (Dama), withdrawal of the mind from things and pursuits that are unrelated to the goal (Uparati), enduring the failures, challenges, difficulties, obstacles and hindrances (Titiksha), having the faith and conviction in the chosen path (Shraddha) and finally having unwavering concentration and always continuously thinking about the goal to be achieved (Samadhana).

Mumukshutva is the burning desire and extreme passion for succeeding. It is refusing to give up and having an intense longing to achieve the desired goal.

Seeker of the Silent Awareness or anyone seriously pursuing the desired goal needs to make a relentless effort to acquire all the above said four-fold qualification taught to us by the Vedic masters.

The website of Swami Shivananda had some unique insight about the Sadhana (effort). It said if one constantly contemplates on the Sentient Life Energy and continuously tries to be in the Silent Awareness then one can succeed quickly without too much Sadhana or effort. Such a person automatically gets one by one all the virtues listed in this section. That means instead of putting a lot of time and effort in acquiring all the qualifications to reach the goal, the easier, smarter and quicker method is to try to directly reach the goal first of being in Silent Awareness, then all the virtues and good qualities get acquired automatically.

Purusharthas – Goal of Human Life

Chaturvidha Purusharthas (four objects of human pursuit) are **DH**arma (duty and righteousness), **AR**tha (wealth), **KA**ma (desire) and **MO**ksha (liberation). Purusharthas are mentioned in the Surya Upanishad of Atharva Veda.

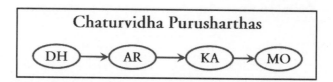

Chaturvidha means four, **Purusha** means an individual or person, and **Artha** means objective, goal, aim, purpose or pursuit. So, **Purusharthas** means the "objects of human pursuit" or "ideal goals of an individual" or "purpose of human life". One is supposed to diligently follow the first three, then the last one, the most important, Moksha (liberation), gets granted automatically.

Purusharthas emphasize the development of morals, ethics and values, and guide the humanity to lead a fulfilled, satisfyingly balanced, meaningful life at the deepest and the most holistic level.

Dharma – Duty and Righteousness

Dharma (DH) is the ethical basis on which we live our life, being conscious in one's actions, words and thoughts. The intention behind any action matters most. The complete meaning of Dharma encompasses duty, responsibility, ethics, morality, righteousness, truth, and respecting the law of the land. The Dharma should not be compromised with at any cost and under any situation.

Dharma forbids shirking of one's responsibility. We have to accept the various responsibilities we have and do the required duties as a parent, child, sibling, relative, friend, colleague, employee, professional, business owner, citizen and finally as a human being.

Dharma promotes love, compassion, empathy, helpful nature, sensitivity to the needs of others and meaningful interaction with the society.

Artha – Wealth

Artha (AR) means "wealth" and the same word also implies "meaning" and one should give value to both the interpretations.

Artha is the pursuit of material wealth to have the security and enjoyment of material comfort we need to live in this world with ease and dignity. Artha does not encourage mad greed to run after money and accumulate wealth. Instead, Artha encourages finding a way so that the money runs behind you and enables you to attain such a point in life where there is a constant feeling of abundance, satisfaction and contentment.

Vedanta never says one should not earn. In fact, it encourages that one should earn as much as possible according to one's ability. It becomes possible to earn by choosing a profession that is compatible with one's nature and capabilities. Bhagavad-Gita calls it as "Swadharma" meaning one's nature, one's natural strength, one's natural interest, one's natural ability. When one relies on Swadharma (natural strength), one can perform great feats and achieve great heights. If the work done is not illegal, morally and ethically correct, then it is always helpful, beneficial and serves the society.

Dharma, honesty and righteousness should NOT be compromised at any cost while pursuing Artha (wealth), otherwise, one's life loses the real Artha (meaning). If Dharma is ignored while pursuing Artha and Kama, meaning profit and pleasure respectively, it leads to social chaos. The world's abundant wealth gets accumulated in the hands of a very small percentage of people leaving behind the majority of the mankind suffering from hunger and poverty.

How true have these thoughts proved to be in the modern world? A report on global inequality dated October 13, 2015, from "The Guardian" says that half of the world's wealth is in the hands of 1% of the population.

Scientists, Thinkers, Statesmen, etc., have to wake up and quickly start emphasizing the utmost importance of moral values and ethics right from the Primary School level so that the future generations can reverse the current situation. Subramanya Bharathi, a fiery and revolutionary poet in the Tamil language, expresses his most heartfelt thought by saying that we need to quickly ensure that for the entire humanity *"scarcity becomes scarce"*.

Kama – Desire

Kama (KA) does not mean just sex or lust. Kama means all kinds of desires, be it biological, physical or material. According to Wikipedia, Kama signifies desire, wish, passion, emotions, pleasure of the senses, the aesthetic enjoyment of life and affection or love.

Vedic philosophy recognizes the importance of satisfying basic human desires. For the overall development of a healthy personality, it is important to have sexual satisfaction, procreation and happy married life. But Vedic philosophy also insists that the Kama (desires) be pursued strictly in accordance with the Dharma (righteousness).

The modern materialistic world believes in just "Eat, drink and be merry". But the overindulgence in merrymaking could lead to exhaustion, addiction, greed, lust, detestation, dissatisfaction, disquiet and depression.

Interestingly in a way Vedic philosophy also says, "Eat, drink and be merry" using the Artha (money) earned and without crossing the line of Dharma (honesty). But the intention of Vedic philosophy encouraging us to clearly "indulge" in enjoying what this world has to offer is to finally realize the temporariness and momentariness of such pleasures. The idea is to eventually gain the wisdom and become successful in reducing the desires.

According to Brihad Aranyaka Upanishad (4.4.5), *"You are what your deepest desire is. As is your desire, so is your intention. As is your intention, so is your will. As is your will, so is your deed. As is your deed, so is your destiny"*.

Moksha – Liberation

Moksha (MO) means liberation, freedom or emancipation. Freedom means becoming free from worldly bondage. Extreme bondage is nothing but having a strong selfish ego and one is completely under the grip of Arishadvarga (band of six enemies) and Pancha Kleshas (five defects). Bondage is due to ignorance.

After having grown up, it is inappropriate to have the thinking of a kindergarten kid. One should not bury the head under the sand like an ostrich and be impervious to the realities of life. Even though on several occasions we have attended somebody's funeral, yet we think we are eternal. Rather, we think that our body is eternal. We wish that death never arrives at our door. We love to accumulate and hoard. Desires are never-ending. We are always worried about something. Satisfaction eludes us. Vedic philosophy says, "Come on. Wake up. Take it easy, buddy". The same thing is conveyed in the Katha Upanishad (1.3.14) and Swami Vivekananda immortalized it by saying *"Arise, Awake and Stop Not until the goal is reached"*.

Moksha, the liberation means not overly rejoicing during success or pleasure and not overly whining or grousing or complaining during failure or pain. It is attaining the mental maturity, calmness, steadiness, poise, composure, equanimity, etc., to be not shaken and to treat both favorable and adverse situations in the same manner. It is possible to be in this state only if the ego is dropped. If the ego is strong, then it is impossible to have mental maturity and mental calmness.

After constant practice, establishing to be in the **Silent Awareness,** one would be able to take things as they come. Come what may, one would be unshaken and face any adversity by looking straight at it and endure any difficulty steadfastly like a solid rock.

It is due to ignorance, the ego becomes strong, desires become never ending and to satisfy those desires one has to engage in several actions every single day until the moment of death. A person who has gained the wisdom drops the ego, does not engage in any meaningless action and always blissfully experiences the **Silent Awareness.** Let us examine some Vedic texts that describe such a wise person who is in the state of Moksha, the ultimate goal which is to successfully be in the blissful state of **Silent Awareness,** the Self, the Atman.

Bhagavad-Gita (3.17) says, *"Person who rejoices only in the Atman, who is satisfied with the Atman, who is content to be with the Atman alone, for that person verily there is nothing more to be done".*

Ashtavakra-Gita (16.4) goes still further and calls the person of fewer actions and who is always in Silent Awareness as a Master Idler to whom even blinking is a botheration disturbing the blissful state of existence. *"Happiness only belongs to such a Master Idler to whom even opening and closing of eyelids seems like a painful activity".*

The above verses should not be misconstrued to mean that they are advocating laziness and lethargy. They convey the blissful state experienced by people who have learnt to experience being in Silent Awareness. People who are attached to worldly things are engaged in constant action, the desires are endless and the mind is restless. The wise person who has succeeded in rejoicing being in Silent Awareness is always calm, happy and is not restless. Any action to be performed is done as a duty and gets back to the happy state of being in Silent Awareness.

Purusharthas Summary

Purusharthas advocate value-based living. Everyone is encouraged to have high ambitions and aspirations and is supposed to pursue those goals vigorously with burning desire and sharp focus. At any point in time, we should be following the Dharma and should not compromise our sincerity, integrity and honesty.

One facet of Dharma also talks about four Ashramas which are four age-based life stages. Ashrama Upanishad exclusively discusses the four ashramas and they are also mentioned in Jabala Upanishad (4.1) and Yajnavalkya Upanishad (1.1). They are Brahmacharya (student life), Grihastha (household life), Vanaprastha (retired life) and Sanyasa (renounced life).

Brahmacharya is the bachelor and celibate student life completely focused on education. A student is supposed to gain the knowledge including ethics, morals, values and virtues.

Grihastha is the married life and this stage represents most intense physical, sexual, emotional, occupational, social and material attachments. A human being is supposed to love the family, live the life cheerfully and fulfill one's responsibilities as a parent, spouse, caretaker, breadwinner for the family, etc. Everyone is encouraged to pursue Artha (wealth) and Kama (desires) vigorously without crossing the boundaries of Dharma (righteousness). In this stage, Vedanta urges everyone to fully indulge in the world and enjoy all the worldly pleasures without violating any ethics or morality.

Vanaprastha is the stage where one should contemplate, decide and enter into retirement handing over all the responsibilities to the next generation. Having had a good education and the materialistic life experience in the previous two Ashramas (stages) respectively, in this third stage one is supposed to reflect on the life and gain wisdom. Whatever we considered important and cared for a few decades back which defined our individuality then are no longer considered important in the present. In the same way, whatever we are currently concerned with, which is defining our individuality in the present may not be considered important by us in the next decade. Vedic philosophy is asking us to understand this fact and develop the mental maturity, gain the wisdom to willingly lose the individuality by dropping the ego and become devoid and free of desires and self-centered thoughts.

Reflecting back on the previous Ashrama which is the Grihastha stage, as a householder we get all our comforts from the society. Starting from our everyday food, vegetable, refrigerator, TV, smartphone, car, each and everything we use, has been obtained from the society even though we might have paid for it. A large number of people have worked tirelessly around the year to provide us with all the comforts and they would continue to provide them.

In the Vanaprastha stage, we are supposed to start giving back to the society what we can. We can do charity, philanthropy, educate the poor, adopt a child, children or a village, work to provide health care, give motivational speeches, write to bring the awareness, etc. The idea is that in whatever way we find it convenient and comfortable it is imperative that we give something back to the society which has nurtured and nourished us all along.

Alas, this thinking escapes the materialistic human mind and the human being gets stuck permanently in the Grihastha Ashrama until the end. That means one does not stop working, wants to earn till the end, ignorantly refuses to become free from the hustle and bustle of life, wants to increase comforts and luxuries till the end, wants to increase the possessions and hoard them till the end, remains attached to the worldly objects till the end, remains possessed by the grip of selfishness till the end. This is nothing but not letting go of the ego and Vedanta calls this as Avidya (ignorance) and is the root cause of worries, pain and suffering not just for the individual but for the whole world as the selfish thoughts and deeds increase the distance between the haves and have-nots.

Sanyasa is the stage marked by renunciation of material desires and prejudices. With the experience and the knowledge gained, understanding the temporariness of the pleasure given by the worldly objects, it is about focusing on attaining Moksha (emancipation). It is about finally gaining the wisdom to succeed in dropping the ego and being in Silent Awareness.

Yoga Vasistha – Realm of Freedom

Yoga Vasistha is the science of realizing the **Sentient Life Energy,** the Self, the Atman and is taught by Sage Vasistha to Sri Rama, the Lord himself. The Bhagavad-Gita which happened later is the teaching taught by Lord Sri Krishna to the human being Arjuna. But in Yoga Vasistha the Lord becomes the student receiving the teaching from a human being.

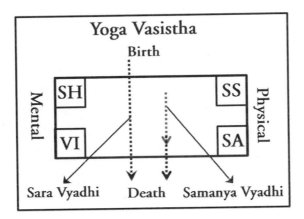

To enter the realm of freedom, there are four gate-keepers or pillars. They are **SH**anti (quietness of mind or self-control), **VI**chara (spirit of inquiry), **SA**ntosha (contentment) and **S**at**S**anga (good company).

Shanti – Calmness

The first pillar **Shanti** (SH) is the calmness obtained after practicing self-control. Any situation, be it favorable or adverse, one needs to face it boldly, firmly and with equanimity. This is possible if the mind is at peace, pure, tranquil, quiet, free from delusion or hallucination, untangled and free from cravings. This state of mind is possible if one drops the ego, continuously contemplates on the **Sentient Life Energy** and strives to be in the **Silent Awareness**. The British philosopher James Allen says, *"The more tranquil a man becomes, the greater is his success, his influence, his power of good. Calmness of mind is one of the beautiful jewels of wisdom".*

Vichara - Enquiry

The second pillar, **Vichara** (VI) is the enquiry and contemplation. Reading and understanding what has been discussed so far in this book, contemplating and examining the validity of the concepts discussed is Vichara (enquiry). Once convinced of the concept, one should strive hard to attain the goal. Thomas Paine, an American Independence activist, says, *"It is error only and not truth that shrinks from enquiry".*

Santosha - Happiness

Santosha (SA) is the happiness obtained due to satisfaction and contentment. The first step to achieve this is to start saying "Enough". If our basic needs are met, we should realize that there are many who are less fortunate than us and be content. The temporariness of the worldly pleasures should be clearly understood, become indifferent to them and be content with what we have. Yoga Vasistha says that there is no delight in this world which is as delightful as contentment. The great Alfred Nobel says, *"Contentment is the only real wealth".*

Satsanga – Good Company

Satsanga (SS) means keeping good company which is to associate with the like-minded people who are pursuing a similar goal as ours. That way the time spent doing all the talking, discussions and efforts would be always related to the goal and helps one progress towards the goal. According to the British writer Izaak Walton, *"Good company in a journey makes the way seem shorter".*

Satsanga does not always mean being with people. Satsanga could also mean the books, lectures, videos, etc., that are related to the goal. Avoiding people whose interests are different from our goal is also a concept of Satsanga.

Sara and Samanya

Sara is the defects and deformities acquired during birth and normally last until the death.

Samanya is the defects, disturbances, disorders and diseases acquired at some point in time in one's life and they may be temporary or sometime might last until death. For example, it could be a painful divorce, one might sustain bodily injuries, become susceptible to diseases like diabetes, hypertension, etc.

Any defect or disease, all the efforts should be definitely made to overcome them. But if it can't be cured, needs to be accepted and endured. No point cribbing about it continuously. But sometimes people instead of accepting the defects, keep worrying about it, continuously curse the fate and in the process unknowingly make themselves perennially unhappy and devastated. Yoga Vasistha warns that such ignorance could cause mental disorders, could end up ruining the whole life and could cause enormous stress, pain and grief to the near and dear ones around us. The Dutch humanitarian, Corrie ten Boom says, *"Worry does not empty tomorrow of its sorrow, it empties today of its strength"*.

Theory of Karma

The word karma is found in Rigveda and significantly in Atharva Veda. Karma Theory is mentioned in Brihad Aranyaka Upanishad (4.4.6). "Karma" literally means "deed" or "act", nothing but the universal principle of cause and effect, action and reaction. According to karma theory, the intent and actions of an individual (cause) influence the future of that individual (effect). Good intent and good deeds contribute to good karma and future happiness, while bad intent and bad deeds contribute to bad karma and suffering.

Karma is closely associated with the idea of rebirth. According to Karma Theory, the quality of present life is due to the karmas done in the past lives and the karma in the present life affects one's future in the current life as well as the nature and quality of future lives.

Naturally, the question arises as to where is the proof for rebirth. We dealt with the same question while discussing the topic Prarabdha Karma and presented some arguments. Let us assume that there is no rebirth and this is the only life. Then there are some compelling arguments against such an assumption.

If there is only one life then with the intelligence of an elementary school kid one would be able to understand that one should go after what one desires with no holds barred. Kill, loot, plunder and anything is fine since one has just this one life. The priority would be to attain the desire of the moment at any cost despite the threat of getting caught and punished. There would be complete social chaos and utter mayhem in the entire world. But the world is not in such a chaotic condition. Why?

When we do a good or noble deed, we feel good. For example, it might be a very simple act of helping a blind person cross the road. If by Nature this is the only life, then this noble deed is against that Nature. One should be robbing the blind person instead of helping. As this is the only life, one should live the life selfishly and why should one care about others?

One should actually feel bad doing a good deed and one should feel really good doing a harmful and criminal act. But the world is not in such a wretched condition. Why?

Doing a virtuous deed, helping someone in need makes one's heart filled with emotion, causes a lump in the throat and makes tears of joy erupt in the eyes. Neuroscience says that such a happy state is associated with the secretion of Serotonin hormone, a happiness chemical. This is the real way of Nature. Why is the way of Nature such if the current life were to be the only life? If doing good does not accrue something good then what is the point of doing them? Then doing bad deeds also does not accrue anything bad and then why one should not continuously indulge in harmful actions?

Though the phenomenon of past and future births cannot be proven with authority, if not anything, belief in Karma Theory only advances the notion of doing good, caring for others, harmonious existence, civilized, human and humane world.

Karma theory does not apply to animals as animals do not have Ego and hence there is no sense of doership. Babies also do not accrue any karma from their actions as their Ego is dormant and not fully developed. As the baby grows up the sense of "I" becomes firm, the doership results and one has to assume the ownership of one's actions irrespective of whether they are good or bad.

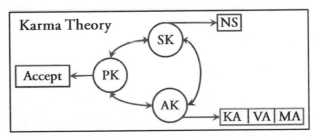

Karma theory identifies that there are three types of karma namely, **Sanchita Karma** (SK), **Prarabdha Karma** (PK) and **Agami Karma** (AK) and these are mentioned in Varaha Upanishad (1.12)

Sanchita Karma (SK) is the pile of karma one has accumulated from all the past lives. This pile containing good and bad fruits has to be exhausted in the future lives. Nishkama Seva (NS) meaning selfless service is encouraged by the Karma Theory to knock off some part of the Sanchita Karma in the current life itself rather than allowing it to fructify in the future life.

Prarabdha Karma (PK) is that small portion extracted from Sanchita that have to be experienced in the current life. We are all born with certain strengths and weaknesses and we need to become aware of them, just accept them and use our natural strengths to our advantage.

Agami or Kriyamana Karma (AK) are the actions we undertake now that result in karma to be experienced sometime in the future of the current life itself or in future lives. Agami is accumulated by MAnasa (mind), VAcha (speech) and KAya (action). If mind, speech and action are good and are resulting in good deeds then there is no problem. But if something not so good thought occurs in the mind, then the Karma Theory says do not bring it to the level of speech or action. If by chance something unpleasant or harmful words have been uttered using speech still it is better to stop at that level rather than bringing it to action. The British philosopher James Allen in his inspirational book "As a Man Thinketh" highlights the importance of good, pure, noble and selfless thoughts. Emphasizing the purity in thinking, the German philosopher Immanuel Kant beautifully says, *"In law, a man is guilty when he violates the rights of others. In ethics, he is guilty if he only thinks of doing so".*

Karma Theory Summary

What the Karma Theory says is if one drops the ego, the doership is not there and any deed done does not accrue any Karma. "I did it", "I made this happen" kind of doership feeling is not there. All the actions get performed with a selfless service mentality. In case of actions performed due to some responsibility, they are executed with a sense of duty and without any egoistic feelings or selfish motives.

According to the Vedic literature, if one becomes successful in dropping the ego and being in Silent Awareness or abiding in the Self, the Atman, all the accumulated pile of Sanchita Karma gets burnt instantly (Mundaka Upanishad 2.2.8). For the one who can successfully be in the Silent Awareness, the ego gets dropped. Hence there is no sense of doership and therefore such a person does not accrue Agami Karma as every action is performed unselfishly. For a person who is firmly established in Silent Awareness even though Prarabdha Karma is still present, such a person is never affected by it because, whether he is confronted with difficulties or with joy, both of them are seen with equanimity. Thus, the Karma Theory applies as long as we have the ego. If the ego is dropped then the effect of karma ceases.

Finally, to conclude, the Karma Theory gives importance to morals, ethics and value-based living so that one can drop the ego and become successful in experiencing the Sentient Life Energy by being in Silent Awareness.

Triguna – Three Qualities

The Bhagavad-Gita which is a Magnum Opus of Vedic Scriptures discusses Triguna in detail. Regarding Bhagavad-Gita, the British philosopher Aldous Huxley says, *"The Bhagavad-Gita is the most systematic statement of spiritual evolution of endowing value to mankind. It is one of the most clear and comprehensive summaries of perennial philosophy ever revealed; hence its enduring value is subject not only to India but to all of humanity".*

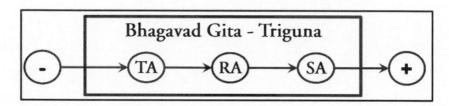

Triguna, the three qualities of the mind are **SA**ttva (Harmony), **RA**jas (Activity) and **TA**mas (Darkness). All three Gunas (qualities) are always present in everyone and at any given time one of the three Gunas will be predominant. The Gunas can never be separated or removed from oneself but can be consciously acted upon to stimulate the increase or decrease of their influence.

Tamas Guna - Darkness

Tamas (TA) is the Guna (quality) that promotes laziness, disgust, materiality, attachment, depression, helplessness, doubt, guilt, shame, boredom, addiction, hurt, sadness, apathy, confusion, grief, dependency, and ignorance. Tamas manifests from ignorance and deludes all beings to be disinterested in Knowledge and makes people dull-witted.

Rajas Guna - Activity

Rajas (RA) is the Guna that promotes energy, euphoria, courage, determination, anger, anxiety, fear, irritation, worry, hyperactivity, restlessness, stress, rumination and chaos. The nature of rajas is of attraction, longing, and attachment. Rajas strongly binds us to the fruits of our work, sense of doership is predominant, urges one to be continuously involved in some activity and the identification with the ego is strong.

Sattva Guna - Harmony

Sattva (SA) is the Guna that promotes the states of harmony, peace, calmness, freedom, wellness, happiness, cheerfulness, joy, delight, bliss, love, compassion, empathy, trust, friendliness, gratitude, satisfaction, fulfillment, fearlessness, focus, self-control, selflessness, equanimity. Sattva is the Guna that causes one to be happy and peaceful.

Triguna Summary

The mind's psychological qualities are highly unstable and can quickly fluctuate between the different Gunas. The predominant Guna of the mind acts as a lens that affects our perceptions and perspective of the world around us. Thus, if the mind is in Rajas, it experiences world events as chaotic, confusing and demanding, and it reacts to those events in a Rajasic way.

According to Bhagavad-Gita, all human beings are combinations of all the three Gunas (qualities) which together make and influence a person's personality. Each personality displays the domination of a certain Guna or a particular combination of Gunas.

It is desirable to have more of Sattva Guna than the Rajas and Tamas as it ensures calm, peace, joy, clarity and focus. Sattva encourages everything to be done under moderation. No over-sleeping or under-sleeping. No overeating or undereating. Balance in relationships, emotions, desires and for that matter balance in everything.

On a subtler level, we need to be mindfully aware of the quality of our thoughts, emotions, beliefs and their effect on us. We may not have a choice about what thoughts and emotions show up, but we do have a choice about which ones we need to pay attention to.

Understanding the Gunas helps us to see things more clearly. It helps to understand the quality of our health, thoughts, actions, and the things with which we engage. Then it is all about making conscious choices on what thoughts we pay attention to and how we act.

Learning to love and delight in Sattva makes one respect morals and values, allows the dropping of the ego and enables the experience of Sentient Life Energy by being in Silent Awareness.

Sadhana Summary

Guru shows the pupil the path of Sadhana (effort). The Vedic literature explains the Sadhana in detail and shows us how to make the effort.

Sadhana Chatushtaya, the four-fold qualifications show us that first we should develop Viveka (reasoning) so that we clearly do the planning and understand what we are aspiring for. Whatever be the goal, Viveka helps us understand the task at hand and do the meticulous planning to reach the goal. Vairagya (dispassion) is to develop disinterest and disgust towards all the things that are not helpful and are distractions that impede our progress towards the goal. Shad Sampat is the six-fold treasures, the virtuous qualities that help strengthen the will and determination, and propel us towards the goal. Finally, the Mumukshutva is the burning desire, the earnest yearning to attain the goal.

Chaturvidha Purusharthas, the four objects of human pursuit, Dharma (righteousness), Artha (wealth), Kama (desire) and Moksha (emancipation) teach us to live righteously without compromising them, pursue one's ambition as per one's capability and earn as much as possible and from the money earned, fulfill all the needs, desires, comforts and luxuries, and finally realize the fleeting temporariness of all the materialist things and pursuits.

Yoga Vasishta highlights the four gatekeepers, Shanti (calmness), Vichara (enquiry), Santosha (happiness), Satsanga (good company). Shanti is to live life calmly and peacefully. Vichara is to do the necessary contemplation before embarking upon any goal. Santosha is to live happily with satisfaction discarding discontentment. Satsanga is to seek the company of the likeminded people and try to always be in an environment that is conducive towards attaining the desired goal.

Karma Theory highly encourages the value-based living and basically advocates *"what goes around comes around"*. Belief in Karma Theory promotes Universal Brotherhood, harmonious coexistence and civilized living.

Triguna (three qualities) helps us understand the three Gunas (qualities), Sattva, Rajas and Tamas. Tamas signifies laziness and lethargy. Rajas signifies hyperactivity and restlessness. Sattva signifies calmness, peace, happiness and contentment. The objective is to increase the Sattva and ensure that Sattva is more predominant in our personality so that we can radiate happiness all around.

After practicing these ideals, one may learn more from the same Guru or different Gurus and one has to intensify the effort and practice. It is just like a professional sportsperson has many different coaches in the career and keeps improving the skills by trying to always learn something new and intensifying the efforts.

Jnana Marga (path of knowledge) encourages one to understand the concepts clearly before putting in the required effort to attain the goal. Vedic philosophy encourages one to have in-depth and profound knowledge in any field of choice. Knowledge in any field such as Mathematics, Physics or the Vedic scriptures is called Apara Vidya (material or lower knowledge) by Mundaka Upanishad (1.4–1.5). Only after possessing in-depth knowledge and excelling in Apara Vidya one becomes eligible to succeed in attaining the Para Vidya (real or higher knowledge) which is succeeding in dropping the ego and being in Silent Awareness. Becoming an expert in Apara Vidya sharpens the intellect and prepares the instrument which is the intellect, fit enough to gain and grasp the Para Vidya.

Once the Sadhana (effort) is intense, the knowledge is complete, the Para Vidya is gained and then the sincere seeker becomes eligible to take a quantum jump.

Quantum Jump to Blissful Life

The **Quantum Jump** is nothing but successfully dropping the ego and enjoying the experiencing of **Sentient Life Energy** by being in **Silent Awareness**. Such a person is called Jivan Mukta (Liberated Soul), Jnani (Knower, Wise), Enlightened, Self-Realized, etc. Bhagavad-Gita calls such a person as Sthitha Prajna (Stable Minded). Such people view and treat every aspect of life equally. They do not overly rejoice during favorable situations nor do they overly complain during adverse situations. They are equanimity and tranquility personified, always exuding love, compassion, empathy and happiness.

Epilogue

"Happiness cannot be traveled to, owned, earned, worn or consumed.
Happiness is the spiritual experience of living every minute with love,
grace, and gratitude."

– Denis Waitley

In the overview section, we saw the "Chart of Blissful Life", unique of its kind, as it tries to capture the essence of the Vedic philosophy in a single page. The chart highlights the three main components, The Mind, Vivekas (reasoning) and the Sadhana (effort).

In the first chapter, "The Mind", we saw the kind of thoughts that occur in the mind and the various factors that influence the thinking of the mind. Research acknowledges the presence of "Unconscious Bias" that affects the thinking of the mind. Vedic literature tries to go into detail to look at the factors influencing the mind. Amazingly the thoughts of the mind always revolve around Vyakti (person), Vastu (object), Vishaya (topic) and Ghatana (incident). Our personality is shaped by the combination of Prarabdha Karma (inherent capabilities), Vasanas (inherent tendencies), Environment, Education and Experience. Then there are Arishadvargas (band of six enemies) and Pancha Kleshas (five poisons) that we need to be wary of, as they affect the thinking of the mind. Finally, we understand that it is not the mind that is the culprit. The mind is just an instrument. Ego is the real culprit. The stronger the ego, more the number of thoughts and more the restlessness of the mind. Being aware of this and taking the necessary steps to reduce the ego makes the mind calm and the life becomes more peaceful and meaningful.

The second chapter explained various Vivekas (reasonings) to understand and unravel the Sentient Life Energy. Drig-Drishya Viveka (seer-seen distinction) showed how this Life Energy is a silent Witness of all our activities. In Pancha Kosha Viveka (science of five sheaths) we got to appreciate the great Vedic Master, Vidyaranya's wit and intellect where he urges us to ignore the five sheaths and become aware of our Awareness or become conscious of our Consciousness. In Traya Avasta Viveka, we saw how Nature is conveying some important messages through our dreamless deep sleep state. In deep sleep state there is no ego and hence it results in Happiness, Peace, Oneness and Unity in Diversity. In Mahavakya Viveka we discussed about the four great sayings found in four different Upanishads. Each one of them in different ways conveyed the same message which is that we are not our name and form; instead, we are the Sentient Life Energy.

In the final chapter Sadhana (effort), we realized the importance of a Guru. We also saw how the revered master Adi Shankara had devised Sadhana Chatushtaya (fourfold qualification) which explains in detail how to put in the effort to achieve the desired goal. Chaturvidha Purusharthas (four goals of human life) describe the ways to live, earn and enjoy the comforts of this world, but all the time without crossing the line of righteousness and honesty. Yoga Vasistha section in its own way advised us to live peacefully, contemplating and enquiring upon the right things, live contentedly and keeping the right company. Karma Theory encourages us to live a life based on morals, ethics, helpfulness, truthfulness, sincerity, honesty and integrity. Bhagavad-Gita explained the Triguna (three qualities) and urged us to increase the Sattva Guna (calmness) within us which promotes calmness, peace, harmony, noble thoughts and deeds.

Vedic literature in various ways persuades us to recognize and acknowledge the presence of the Sentient Life Energy. After understanding, we are required to make the necessary efforts to successfully drop the ego and experience the Sentient Life Energy by being in the Silent Awareness.

Sentient Life Energy

Can anything move on its own without the help of energy? No. In the same way, can the beating of the heart, expansion and contraction of the lungs, functioning of all organs in the body happen on their own without the help of energy? No. Impossible. There is definitely an energy powering all the organs in the entire body including the mind and the intellect which are the subtle organs. That energy is the Life Energy. Unlike all other energies such as electrical, magnetic, light, heat, etc., which are inert, the Life Energy is Sentient. That means the life energy has the ability to know, has Awareness, has Consciousness. The Vedic literature says that the nature of the life energy is Chit meaning Consciousness.

If we just see the light, we understand the light energy. It is that simple. But after knowing about the light energy can we make a person who is born blind understand the light energy? Can we communicate using as many words and examples as needed and somehow make the blind person clearly comprehend the light energy?

It is precisely the same predicament the Vedic literature had to confront. Using words, the Vedic literature is trying to make us understand about an energy which is the Sentient Life Energy and Vedic literature calls it as Chit Shakti (Sentient Energy), Awareness, Consciousness, Self, Atman. Despite the difficulty of making everybody comprehend an energy using mere words, the Vedic literature has done a pretty good job of explaining the Life Energy.

To experience the light energy, we just see it using the eyes as the instrument. To experience the heat energy, we can just feel it using the skin as the instrument. To experience the Life Energy, we need to make use of its Sentience using the calm mind as the instrument. For that sharp intellect is necessary. Since animals do not have this instrument called intellect they cannot realize the Life Energy just like a blind person cannot see the light. If the instrument is present but is not in good condition then also it is of no use. A mirror covered by dust cannot reflect the image properly. Once the dust is removed, then the mirror does its job perfectly. In the same way, our ego acts as a veil and hence obstructs us from experiencing our life energy. Due to our conditioning, we identify ourselves with our name and form because of the ego. This, in turn, generates self-centered thoughts in the mind continuously preventing us from experiencing our **Sentient Life Energy.** Dropping the ego makes the mind calm and enables the experience of the **Sentient Life Energy** by being in **Silent Awareness.**

Practicing and living without compromising on ethics, morals, virtues and values are the essential requirements to succeed in dropping the ego. Regarding morals, the German philosopher Immanuel Kant says, *"Two things awe me most, the starry sky above me and the moral law within me"*. It is impossible to drop the ego if we think and act in a selfish manner.

Starting to say "Enough" is the first step that is necessary to drop the ego. Thinking about the people who are less fortunate than us and thanking the Providence for what we are today, we should firmly resolve to live the rest of our lives with satisfaction and contentment by saying "Enough".

Every comfort of ours such as car, bed, TV, smartphone, watch, clothes, etc., have come from the society. Though we might have paid for the comforts, millions of people are working tirelessly all-round the year to produce those goods to keep the society happy which includes us too. So, the work we do for our living is a very small individual effort adding to the great global cause. We are one global village, one global society mutually helping each other. Vedic philosophy calls it as "Vasudhaiva Kutumbakam" meaning "One Global Family". Such thoughts make way for the sacred "Service Mentality" to become predominant rather than the prevailing capitalistic "Profit Mentality".

Vedic philosophy says that all our pain and suffering are due to the presence of the ego. Because of the ego we very strongly want something and in the same way, we strongly do not want something else. When the dice does not roll our way, then we feel the pain and the suffering starts. If the ego is less or completely dropped, then during the adverse and unfavorable circumstances one would be able to face them bravely or endure them valiantly without losing one's smile, charm and enthusiasm. Thus, the .

purpose of dropping the ego is to discover the Blissful Peace inwardly and radiate joy, love and compassion outwardly. So, to attain Individual Peace let us make the effort needed to drop the ego and experience the Silent Life Energy by being in **Silent Awareness.**

There are no two different electrical energies. In the same way, there is only one and there are no two **Sentient Life Energy.** Bulb, fan, TV, etc., differ in their name and form but are powered by the same electrical energy. All of us differ in our name and form but are powered by the same **Sentient Life Energy.** When we identify ourselves with the **Sentient Life Energy** instead of our name and form, then we would see the same Life Energy in every human being. The result is Peace, Oneness and Unity in Diversity. By dropping the ego and being in **Silent Awareness,** we attain the Individual Peace and then we become eligible to contribute towards establishing Vishwa Shanti (World Peace). The huge defense budgets of all the nations can be cut down by more than half. Police stations in the world could be rendered redundant. The money saved could be diverted for the welfare of the entire mankind. This dream is not utopian. Vedic philosophy says such a golden era of global civilization is very much possible and it is indeed the highest possible pristine way of human existence.

To usher in such a golden era, we need to first acknowledge the presence of Life Energy and understand that its nature is Sentience. Then we need to establish the study of this all-important **Sentient Life Energy** right from the Primary School level along with the paramount importance being given to ethics, values, virtues and morality. The British novelist Clive Staples Lewis says, *"Education without values, as useful as it is, seems rather to make man a more clever devil".* In the present world, in the name of competition, kids see professional sportspersons openly abusing each other hurling all kinds of expletives. We need to make the effort that the future generation is brought up with greater morals and values so that they get to live in a more peaceful and harmonious world. Children should study in detail about the **Sentient Life Energy,** the joy in giving and the importance of values-based living.

Just like Mother's Day or Father's Day, we could celebrate Ego-less Day or Day of Universal Love or Awareness Day. We could have debates, discussions, speeches, songs and engage in all kinds of activities promoting and educating everybody how to enjoy the **Silent Awareness** by dropping the individual egos. We could make school children write essays and give talks on how the world would be if the nations did not have defense ministry, did not have defense armament factories and did not have huge defense budgets. If the nations can afford to reduce their defense expenditure significantly and all those resources could be diverted for the betterment of the mankind how peaceful and blissful this world would be. All the police stations in the world could be rendered redundant. Overnight we will not get there, but that is clearly the final human destination. This dream is not utopian; in fact, the Vedic philosophy says it is the highest state of human existence possible if only we could use our minds wisely and drop our puny egos. This is what Vedic philosophy means by "Loka Kshema" meaning Global Wellbeing and *"Sarve Jana Sukhino Bhavantu"* meaning let all the people of the world be happy.

In this book, we have tried to explain the Vedic philosophy in as simple manner as possible so that it is easy to understand which is vital. We have stressed the importance of dropping the ego and also described how one could go about dropping the ego. We have emphasized the importance of morals, ethics, values, contentment, mental purity and selflessness without which dropping of ego is not possible. Finally, we have suggested a simple, yet powerful and effective meditation technique prescribed by Revered Ramana Maharshi to experience the **Sentient Life Energy** by "being" in **Silent Awareness.**

The main intention of this book is to bring in mass awareness about the presence of the **Sentient Life Energy** which is providing us with the life every moment. Once the existence of the Life Energy is acknowledged, it would pave the way for the mass enlightenment to happen so that the burning desire is ignited in everyone's heart to experience the **Sentient Life Energy.** Then everyone can put in the required effort wholeheartedly and succeed in experiencing the Sentient Life Energy by being in **Silent**

Awareness. Dropping the ego, living with contentment and satisfaction, living with high ethical and moral standards, and enjoying being in **Silent Awareness,** guarantee stress-free, blissful Individual Peace and make the Global Peace with harmonious coexistence a distinct possibility. We hope that this book becomes a humble candle and succeeds in lighting innumerous hearts with the light of Knowledge, Happiness, Peace, Oneness, Love and Compassion.

According to Vedic philosophy, these are the grand exemplary ideals that can be definitely attained by just dropping the ego and experiencing the blissful **Sentient Life Energy** by being in **Silent Awareness.** When such an ultimate success can be achieved, the same Vedic principles and teachings could very well be applied to succeed in attaining any desired goal in any chosen field. Vedic philosophy is not about some belief or dogma. It is about better living, meticulous planning and focused effort to achieve the desired goal.

Vedic philosophy through Purusharthas (goals of human life) encourages us to push the envelope, test one's limits, venture into unchartered territories and using one's ability achieve great feats. It encourages everyone to earn as much as possible according to one's ability and enjoy all the comforts and luxuries that money can buy. But the only important condition is that Dharma (righteousness) should not be compromised at any cost. That means great importance is given to honesty, sincerity, integrity, morals, ethics and value-based living. Vedic philosophy says only a King can renounce, a beggar cannot. After complete indulgence in worldly comforts and enjoyments, it would be possible to realize the fleeting temporariness of the enjoyment they provide. Only at that point, it would be possible to turn the mind inwards and seek for the experience of the **Sentient Life Energy** by being in **Silent Awareness.**

About the Authors

Dr. Yogi Devaraj is the founder President of "Swami Vivekananda Yoga Research & Holistic Health Trust". His qualifications are M.A. (Economics), L.L.B. and in his professional life, he retired as the Manager of State Bank of Mysore. For more than 20 years he has been passionately pursuing his interests in Yoga, obtained the degrees MSc, M.Phil and has been awarded Hon. Doctorate in Yoga. Dr. Devaraj is an expert in Yoga Therapy and counselling and has helped thousands of people recover from stress related disorders. He has trained a number of Yoga teachers and Yoga therapists on behalf of the Govt. of India through SVYASA Yoga University. As a renowned Yoga expert and an International speaker, he has conducted several successful Yoga camps all over the world.

✉@ yogi.devaraj@sentientlifeenergy.com

Arun Kumar is an Engineer by qualification, a software veteran with 30 years of experience. He holds 6 patents, all related to software engineering and 2 more are in pending status. He has been part of design and development of several successful software products that have been sold and used worldwide. He is currently working as a Principal Software Engineer at Cisco Systems, Bangalore. At Cisco, along with his junior colleague, he has successfully innovated and implemented a Timeseries Graph Database. It is a Graph Database that stores Vertices (entities) and Edges (relationships between entities) but is also capable of instantaneously providing the snapshot of the database for any given point in time. It is being used for analyzing the network structure, traffic, user interests, utilization of {bandwidth, applications, network devices} etc. Besides software, for the past 15 years, he has been intensely pursuing his interests in Vedic philosophy and is an ardent reader of Indian Vedic literature.

 arun.kumar@sentientlifeenergy.com

 https://www.linkedin.com/in/arunkumar8hudku

Venugopala C.V. is a multi-faceted personality. A Mechanical Engineer by qualification has worked as a software delivery manager with well-known multi-nationals like IBM, Verisign, HCL Perot to name a few. Besides, he is a writer by passion and a personality development mentor by choice. He is also a Technical Advisor for Affordable Housing & Urban Development Society by invitation. He has authored a book titled "Empower Your Mind and Succeed".

 venugopala@sentientlifeenergy.com

 https://www.linkedin.com/in/Venugopala-CV

☛ www.sentientlifeenergy.com